OVERFLOWING LIFE

OVERFLOWING LIFE

ROBERT C. FROST, PhD

Logos International
Plainfield, New Jersey

OVERFLOWING LIFE

*All quotations from Scripture
are taken from the King James Version
unless otherwise indicated.*

Library of Congress Catalog Card Number
72-146696

We wish to acknowledge the use of the following publications:
Wuests, *An Expanded Translation*, Eerdmans
Amplified Bible, Zondervan
Jerusalem Bible, Doubleday
Living Gospels, Tyndale House
Living Books of Moses, Tyndale House
Lamsa version, Holman
Living Letters, Tyndale House
Weymouth, Harper and Row

Dedicated in love and devotion

to my family

Ruth
     Robert, Jr.
          Betsy
              Alicia
                   Sharon

CONTENTS

Foreword   7

Preface 11

 1. Prayer in the Spirit 17

 2. The Spirit and God's Word 29

 3. The Spirit and Our Witness 33

 4. Fellowship in the Spirit 39

 5. The Spirit-Filled Home 49

 6. Truth and Error: Principles 69

 7. Truth and Error: Problems 85

 8. The Spirit of Holiness 111

 9. The Spirit of Joy and Peace 121

10. The Spirit of Love 125

Appendix 129

OVERFLOWING LIFE

The Holy Spirit is a very practical person who desires to direct the power of God into every area of our personal lives. The graces and gifts of the Spirit become streams of life by which Jesus Christ sets us free to become ourselves in Him. In this book various aspects of our devotional life and personal ministry are discussed within a charismatic framework. The unique privileges and problems related to the Spirit-filled home and community are considered in a practical forthright fashion. The principles by which the believer can discern between truth and error are presented within a Christ-centered perspective. The themes discussed are all based upon both practical and personal experience in the charismatic movement which currently is reaching every area of Christendom the world over.

PREFACE TO OVERFLOWING LIFE

The chapters related to our life and walk in the Spirit in the author's first edition of *Aglow with the Spirit* have in this volume been increased in number and content and published under a different title. The second edition of *Aglow with the Spirit* deals with the Baptism of Jesus in the Holy Spirit and forms the foundation upon which this volume is based. The two books complement each other and are designed to aid the believer in understanding his spiritual privileges and responsibilities as an earthly member of God's heavenly family!

Some seven years have elapsed since the first edition was written. Several areas of vital interest and need have become evident as time and travel both in the United States and abroad have provided the necessary opportunities for observation and evaluation. There is a growing appreciation for the true concept of Christian community within the charismatic context. As with the first community, described in the opening chapters of Acts, the life of the fellowship is related to the twofold function of unity within and witness without. In this, Christ's intercessory prayer finds its fulfillment. "Father I pray that they might be one . . . that the world might believe!" (John 17:21).

The "climax of the ages" as envisioned by the Apostle Paul is now coming into view! (Ephesians 1:9-11, *Amplified Bible*). The theme of this new edition relates to this divine desire which our Heavenly Father has conceived for His earthly family. God is yet going to have a people for His name!

The Holy Spirit is most practical, and the heavenly ideal finds its realizations as our own earthly families are claimed for God's divine purpose. Satan has intensified his attack upon the Christian family for He recognizes the power which can be generated by "two or three" truly united together in Jesus' name! For this reason a chapter on the Spirit-filled home has been added to the text.

Another area which the Enemy is exploiting relates to error and deceptive distractions which divide members of the Father's family and weaken the witness of the Christian community as a whole. Two extensive chapters on the principles and problems of discernment and deliverance have been included to meet this rather urgent need. The concept of the cross as realized in our daily lives is emphasized as a necessary part of the Christian's armor.

Every chapter has been expanded with additional insights and illustrations which have developed during the intervening years. Each has been designed to help the newly Spirit-baptized believer to become soundly grounded in God's principles and purposes for His people. Both heavenly privileges and earthly problems of the Spirit-filled life are discussed in a practical and personal way.

It is the desire of the author that the message contained in the following pages will reach the heart of the reader in a most life-refreshing way. It is with great expectation and glorious hope that together we claim the full will and purpose of our Heavenly Father for these exciting and important days just before us.

May we ever be filled-to-overflowing Christians with the life-giving Spirit of our wonderful Lord. This is our destiny for Jesus promised that if we continued to believe in Him as the Scriptures have said, out of our innermost beings would continually flow spiritual rivers of living water (John 7).

The author gratefully acknowledges the secretarial assistance of Mrs. C.E. (Mary) Gonser, and Mrs. G.W. (Shirley) Nelms, as well as my wife, Ruth.

OVERFLOWING LIFE

Prayer in the Spirit

After you are filled with the Holy Spirit, you will find a whole new dimension opening up in your Christian life. Your initial experience is but the *beginning* of an exciting and wonderful adventure in the Lord. You have launched out into the "life abundant." As you mature in your experience, you need never lose its freshness. *The Holy Spirit is the never-failing Spirit of hope and expectation.*

This does not mean that there will not be trials and even persecution. In fact, the power of Satan will be felt as never before. But, you have a heavenly source in the Holy Spirit who by faith will release the power, wisdom, and love of Christ through your life each day.

Therefore, begin each day by giving the day back to God and fully committing yourself to the Holy Spirit who desires to equip, teach, and use you for His glory. Expect something new from God each day *for* you; that *through* you, He may draw others to Himself.

Faith is characterized by its object. The object of our faith is a great God. *Great faith will have great expectations!* Begin to believe for God's daily working in your life in ways that will be as wonderful and amazing as He is. "Eye hath not seen, nor ear heard, neither have entered into the heart of man, the things which God hath prepared for them that love him. But God hath revealed them unto us by His spirit" (I Cor. 2:9-10). "The things" referred to in the above passage are the "all things" which pertain to Jesus which the Holy Spirit will show unto us (John 16:15). In other words Jesus is going to become progressively more real to you than He has ever been before. You will know more and more of *His* love and *His* power and of *His* wisdom in your life! This is what it means to live a Spirit-filled life. "If we live in the Spirit, let us also walk in the Spirit" (Gal. 5:25). The spiritual walk of the Christian has direction. We are going somewhere. The "somewhere" is really to "someone" . . . Jesus Christ!

Let us see how the Holy Spirit desires to bring life to Christian experience in the areas of prayer, Bible study, and witness. We will begin with prayer.

A pastor once exclaimed right after receiving the fullness of God's Spirit in praise, "Why, prayer won't be a chore anymore!" He was absolutely right. The Holy Spirit is the Spirit of prayer. When we by faith close ourself off to pray "with God's Spirit," we are entering into a most meaningful experience. There is indeed a refreshing and a release. *Prayer should be as alive as is the God to whom we pray.* One of the most deadening things in Christian experience is "saying prayers," instead of talking to God.

I can remember during "circle prayers" awaiting my turn and carefully rehearsing what and how I was going to pray. Occasionally, someone else would "steal" my prayer before my turn came, and I would be left high and dry and at a loss for words. I somehow suspect that my part of the prayer circle was about as unsatisfactory to God as it was empty for me. I have since discovered that I was not alone in such frustrations, although this is really of little comfort. How hollow our prayers can sometimes be! It is the desire of the Holy Spirit to fill our lives with praise and prayer. He neither slumbers nor sleeps and prays without ceasing. *If we are filled with God's Spirit, we are filled with never-failing prayer!*

By faith we can "tune in" to the Spirit of prayer and "with Him" lift heavenward our confessions, intercessions, petitions, and praise. No wonder Paul encourages us to pray "with our spirit as moved by His Spirit" (I Cor. 14:15) Wuest's Expanded Translation). This truth is further reinforced in Ephesians 6:18 and Jude 20 where we are admonished to pray "in, by means of, through" the Holy Spirit that we might stand strong and be built up in the most holy faith (various translations).

Praying in tongues and with our understanding is an active expression of *a living faith in a living God.* One of the most exciting

18

experiences of the Spirit-filled life is that God really does answer prayer. To *say* it is one thing; to *see* it is another. If we say it in faith, we will see it in life . . . our life!

A professional coleague of mine has just recently been filled with the Holy Spirit. A brush fire was threatening the home of a mutual friend early one Sunday afternoon. An appeal for prayer was made, and we all responded by seeking God's protection for their home. The flames were ehecked and their home was saved. My colleague later told us of their prayer experience at the time. They had taken time out from the activities of Sunday dinner and had prayed an earnest but short prayer for God's intervention. He immediately felt that God had heard and would act accordingly. They rejoiced but were not surprised to learn of the outcome. "It's a funny thing," he said, "but before being filled with God's Spirit, I never would have had that kind of faith." Jesus is the Author and Finisher of our faith (Heb. 12:2). *The Holy Spirit of faith simply makes Him more real to us!*

OUR PRAYER OF PRAISE

There are several different expressions to prayer. We have already mentioned the purpose and power in praise. *Praise is a very positive expression of our faith!* It should be a continual part of our daily experience. Our last thoughts at night and our first thoughts in the morning should be those of praise to God. As a compass needle immediately swings to the north when distracting forces are removed, so should our minds go fleeting back to God in worship all through the day as we move from one mental task to another. A great deal of God's power can quickly be compressed into our lives as periodically we lift our voices, audibly or inaudibly as the occasion may allow, to Him in divinely directed praise. There is great edifying power in praying in tongues all throughout the day. Here is one way we can repeatedly "tune in" to the unceasing Spirit of praise who faithfully fills our lives with His presence.

Someone once raised the question, "Do you claim to be able to pray in tongues anytime you want to? Isn't that like turning God on and off according to your whim and fancy?" I had never thought of the abiding privilege of Spirit-inspired prayer quite in that sense before, and I had no desire to be turning Him "on and off" like a water faucet. I asked the Lord about this. His reply was simple and direct as is so often the case. "Don't worry about it," He responded, "I am always on! . . . You are the one who needs to be turned on in faith. My unceasing Spirit of prayer will ever be ready to respond." I have never worried about the question since. God is always faithful and He is always worthy of our praise.

Some time ago we received a letter from a lady and her husband whom it had been our privilege to lead into the fullness of the Holy Spirit. She was describing the new joy that God had brought to their lives and how Thanksgiving Day had been the most wonderful Thanksgiving they had ever spent together.

Then she shared something I will never forget. "Do you notice," she said, "that we seem to be saying 'Praise God' more since we 'received'? The words 'Praise God' flow so easily from our lips, and these words seem to be definitely connected with our heart. Anyway, I seem to get a little 'pang' when I say it."

This really touched my heart. In fact, it brings tears to my eyes just to think about it again. I know what she was talking about! The Holy Spirit has a way of linking our hearts with Jesus when we praise Him that brings a thrill to this earthly life of ours. To know the touch of Jesus is to be spoiled for anything else as far as *real* joy in this world is concerned. How, apart from His Spirit, could we ever praise Him as we should?

Praising God in tongues can become a sensitive thermometer for the Spirit-filled Christian. Only a life filled with God will continually want to praise Him. Conversely, one of the first dimensions to go in a life where the Holy Spirit has been grieved will be the desire to praise God. The Spirit of worship has been quenched. Our communion with the Holy Spirit around the praiseworthiness of God's Son has been broken. *Even the slightest sin unconfessed will dampen our desire to praise the Lord!*

I have found in my own life that this is one of the ways the Holy Spirit will most quickly and specifically bring to my attention some sin that needs to be confessed. It is impossible to praise God in tongues and be irritated at one's children at the same time. God has a way of desiring our praise in the midst of most "earthy" situations. *Any attitude of heart or mind which robs God of the praise He deserves is sin.* As soon as it is confessed in faith, our communion with the Holy Spirit in Christ is restored. So is our joy and peace in the Lord. In this way the purifying power of praise can find a very practical function in our daily lives.

Praise also is often the fountainhead from which other manifestations of the Spirit stream forth. At the close of a morning worship service where I had spoken, an elderly lady approached me for prayer. Symptoms of a former illness involving cancer were returning and she requested the ministry of healing. I felt no great surge of faith and was a little reluctant to pray before confessing the faithful presence of the Lord. I suggested we worship God together and allow Him to inhabit our praises with His life-giving power. As we began to pray in the Spirit, God moved upon her with such force I was afraid she was going to fall over. Our faith reached forth for her healing and I immediately ministered to her with the laying on of hands. Her symptoms disappeared like shadows flee from the light and warmth of the early morning sun. How faithfully the Son of righteousness arises with healing in His wings when beckoned by the praises of God's people (Mal. 4:2).

Her daughter than came forward and confessed her need for deliverance from the bondage of fear and depression. As we prayed, I encouraged her to respond to the Spirit in worship, and she immediately broke forth in a heavenly tongue glorifying and magnifying God. Needless to say, the Lord exchanged her spirit of heaviness for the garment of praise! (Isa. 61:3).

One final illustration came to my attention shortly after the first edition of this book was published. One of my students joyfully told me of an older friend who was in the hospital with a painful spinal problem. As he was reading alone in his room, the simplicity of worshiping God by His Spirit in faith, regardless of circumstances, reached his heart. With great gladness he lifted his voice in spontaneous praise, completely lost in the holy wonder of God's glorious presence. At that moment the oil of joy became God's healing balm as well, and he was instantly delivered from his infirmity and subsequently discharged from the hospital. What a beautiful confirmation of God's Word that He does indeed inhabit the praises of His people! (Ps. 22:3).

OUR PRAYER OF CONFESSION

We now rather naturally come to another expression of prayer, that of confession. *Confession in prayer must always be of a twofold nature, negative and positive.* "Negatively" we confess our sins, mistakes, failures, imperfections, and great need. We readily confess all that we are not. And, in ourselves, we are nothing! Then in faith and with rejoicing we "positively" confess our Savior, His forgiveness, His perfection, and our righteousness in Him. We readily confess all that He is. And, in Him, we have everything!

Satan is very subtle and will always try to limit our confession to repeated negatives. Sometimes he will point an accusing finger at some defect in our life and through continual condemnation drive us to despair and discouragement. Our testimony at such a time is completely neutralized, and God's will for our lives frustrated. This is one way Satan endeavors to undermine our witness for Christ. *We should be prepared to overcome such an evil Spirit of despair by actively presenting a positive confession of our faith.*

An occasion in our own lives required just such an expression of our faith before the darkness of discouragement was defeated. I had been invited to speak at a Christian Advance meeting in Riverside, California. The weather was hot, and by late afternoon our entire family was tired and a little on the edgy side. To make matters worse, we lost our way, and I was growing fearful that we might be late. As time progressed, I became more irritable within and sharp-spoken without. Before long, however, the Holy Spirit faithfully impressed me with how grievous this was to the Lord. I had no sooner confessed my failure than this barbed thought flashed through my mind: *How can I stand before an audience tonight and minister the peace and joy of the Lord when my own life has been such an obvious contradiction?* My heart sank in despair and a fear bordering on inner panic overwhelmed me. God's faithful Spirit then brought a word of hope to my remembrance. Had God not said that "if we confess our sins, he is faithful and just to forgive us our sins, and to cleanse us from all unrighteousness"? (I John 1:9). This meant simply that we would again be clean and fit vessels for God's Spirit to fill. God said so! I immediately made this positive confession with my full understanding quickened by the Holy Spirit. As a further expression of faith I moved on into devotional tongues allowing this release to be a means of "washing from my life" the inner tensions and confusion. As the Holy Spirit used this means of grace to edify my life, an awareness of His peace brought a quietness to my troubled soul.

That night, God's hand of evident blessing was upon His Word and in a most encouraging way God confirmed to me again the overcoming power which He brings to a positive confession of faith. *The Holy Spirit will always honor a positive confession of God's Word!* If we confess anything less than this, the Spirit is grieved and we quench His work and witness in our lives. This is the reason some prayers seem so gray and lifeless.

OUR PRAYER OF INTERCESSION

Another dimension in our prayer is related to intercession. Here, by faith, we allow the Holy Spirit to *identify* ourselves with a personal need, and at the same time to *identify* ourselves with the divine supply which is in the Lord Jesus. The intercessory prayer of faith bridges heaven and earth on behalf of someone that God has laid upon our hearts. *We become God's link of love.* Jesus was and is an intercessor. If we are to become like Him, we, too, will allow the Spirit of intercession to move us in prayer.

Praying in tongues gives intercessory prayer a powerful dimension. Perhaps at no other time do we more keenly feel the limitations of our understanding. The force of our prayer is weakened by the fact that we do not know how to pray as we ought. How good of God to provide a way which bypasses the limitations of our minds and of our speech! We know that divinely expressed intercession will always be in keeping with God's divine purposes. This provides a real safeguard for our prayers and allows our faith to find full expression without reservations concerning His will.

How easy it is for us sometimes to program somebody else's life! We begin to project into our prayer what we think would be God's will for their situation. Just recently we have seen the Lord answer our prayers for someone in a most unusual way. It was something we never would have anticipated. God very clearly showed us the danger of limiting Him by tending to rely upon our understanding alone. God works in ways which to man are mysterious. *Praying in tongues is one way that the mysteries of God can be spoken without passing through the restricting filter of our minds.*

A wife and mother in her early fifties approached me at the end of a Bible class and requested that we pray for her inner needs concerning a serious personal problem in her family. We had prayed with her some months earlier and God had brought an inner healing to her life and there were evidences of a healing work in her home as well.

Recent reverses, coupled with physical distress, had painfully pressed her to a place of lonely desperation which prompted her plea for help from me and some of her sisters in the Lord who had remained behind after the class had concluded. Not sensing the seriousness nor the intensity of her inner anguish, I encouraged her to keep praising the Lord, with a little feeling of impatience concerning her lack of faith. How cruel and void of compassion we sometimes can be with others, even while endeavoring to minister God's Word! I have discovered *the truth can kill as quickly as error if it is not ministered in love and with Christian grace!*

The Holy Spirit sharply reproved my soul within and I realized God wanted us to intercede on behalf of our sister without further discussion. (There are times when prayer is preferable to words.) We gathered around her and began to pray with both faith and feeling for her personal need. As we were thus holding her up in prayer, she suddenly collapsed to the floor . . . into the arms of Jesus! As we knelt by her prostrate form, I realized she had reached her emotional, physical, and spiritual limits, so pressed was she in soul. *Fortunately, our limits are not God's!*

We continued to intercede for her and encouraged her to allow the Holy Spirit to intercede on her behalf. She began praying in her heavenly tongue with spiritual groanings that could not otherwise have been expressed. *There are times when only the Holy Spirit Himself can completely encompass the inner anguish of our souls.* She had come for spiritual ministry, and the faithful intercession of the Holy Spirit prevailed.

A powerful surge of spiritual authority rose up within us, and we challenged Satan to his face in the almighty name of Jesus! We rebuked the spirit of depression and released our sister into the joy and peace of her Lord. Her whole expression changed, and she triumphantly arose as a true daughter of the King! It was like watching Lazarus come forth from the tomb! The resurrection power of Him who ever liveth to make intercession for us had prevailed again (Heb. 7:25). We all joined together in praise and thanksgiving for God's abundant grace and mercy for our sister. *There is perhaps no more beautiful or needed ministry than that of intercessory prayer* ! (Isa. 59:16).

OUR PRAYERS OF PETITION

Lastly, let us consider our prayers of petition. Jesus said that if we would ask anything in His name He would do it that the Father would be glorified in the Son (John 14:13). The "anything" is qualified in a twofold way. First of all, *we must present the name of Jesus with our petition.* That name represents who He is and what He has accomplished for us.

The name also represents who we are in Him! When we were born into God's family through the life of Jesus as our Savior, we not only inherited His nature but also received His name. We have been baptized into His body and are accepted in the beloved and thereby bear His name for God's glory. There is legal authority in the name of Jesus and the power of the Holy Spirit to execute that authority. As we move in faith, our prayers should become as strong as those that Jesus prayed!

"As my Father hath sent me, even so send I you" (John 20:21).

Secondly, *what we ask for must be so related to Jesus that it will bring glory to the Father.* In other words, everything in our lives, whether large or small, earthly or heavenly, people, places, or things, is to revolve around God's Son. Every prayer must place Jesus in its center! If we are sure of this, then we can ask anything in all confidence.

Sometimes God honors our prayer of faith by giving us the desires of our hearts rather than the petitions we have requested. God-given desires can occasionally be misdirected when it comes to the way in which we may anticipate their fulfillment. Praying in the Spirit that our understanding may be clear concerning the timing and fashion of God's answer is important. Our natural minds have a peculiar way of fastening onto an immediate answer which has personal appeal. Our prayers then follow in line unless we recognize the little red flags the Holy Spirit raises as warning signals.

A student of mine was having great difficulty in mastering the prescribed courses for his premedical major. We had talked and prayed together with little result as far as the academic area of his life was concerned. After several semesters, it was obvious that medicine was most definitely not his calling. Yet he seemed reluctant to consider any other alternatives for his life. As we shared further together, the following picture finally emerged:

He and one of his close friends had a strong and sincere desire to serve God and be used of Him in ministering to others. They agreed together in prayer to make the medical profession the direction for their lives. The young man's parents were proud and pleased, and subsequently allowed no other alternative to be raised for possible consideration. The two students often prayed together, but only the other boy satisfactorily completed his course and subsequently was accepted into medical school.

It was apparent that God was trying to speak, but a preconceived set of mind precluded the possibility of a hearing until the circumstances forced a confrontation with reality. As we talked together, we recognized that the boy's desire to share the love of God with people was put into his heart by the Lord. He excelled in sports and worked with underprivileged youngsters at the local Y.M.C.A. He also enjoyed history but had never seriously considered teaching in either of these areas because his goal had already been rigidly set.

God broke a heavy yoke that day as a young man made the glorious discovery that the Lord could answer the desire of his prayers in a way somewhat different than he had petitioned! He opened himself in faith and expectation to a whole new direction in life for Christian service. A teaching major in history with a minor in physical education fitted his personality and God's will for his life like green fits the color of grass.

Did God answer his prayer? Yes, in a far more wonderful way for him than he previously had ever thought possible. Maybe we all should examine our petitions more carefully before we try to force an answer where it was never intended to fit. What freedom and faith our prayers can have when we finally allow God Himself to shape the answer for the need!

Finally, our prayers of petition should never become commonplace. We may pray in common places but always with an awareness that God is near and hears every word. Some time ago my wife attended a small prayer-and-share group in Tulsa, Oklahoma. Following the prayer time, one of the ladies approached my wife and said, "As you were praying, I saw Jesus standing beside you with His hand upon your head." When she shared this with me, I couldn't help but think that God in His grace sometimes pushes back the curtains of this earthly life of ours just enough for us to see how very close He really is. Many of the prayers offered that night have already been answered. God really does answer prayer!

THE PREVAILING POWER OF PERSISTENT PRAYER

The Adversary will ever seek to place a seal upon our lips when it comes to our prayer and praise. He is well aware of the power which is released when by faith we strike through to this mighty stream of God's Spirit. Subtle and devious are Satan's ways and we need to recognize the methods which he employs.

In the early days of our life in the Spirit the Lord taught me an unforgettable lesson. A group of college students who had recently been Spirit-baptized were meeting weekly in our home. On one such evening I was awaiting their arrival in a spirit of expectant prayer and praise. How thankful we were for all that God had so sovereignly been doing in our midst! Soon the time for their arrival came, but no one made an appearance. My praise began to dwindle and finally faded out altogether. Time moved on and the silent doorbell became an object of irritation and resentment. Dark thoughts flooded my mind concerning the unkind and unfair remarks some people had made concerning the character and conduct of our fellowship. *Why didn't they come and see for themselves, or talk firsthand with some of the students whose lives*

26

had been so graciously changed? I wondered.

It seemed that some cruel, restraining influence had discouraged the meeting as planned. I was deeply and personally distressed at heart. At this point the Holy Spirit reminded me that a few days earlier He had revealed to me that God's children could face any situation with the faith, hope, and love of Jesus. As if in contrast, my mind had been darkened by doubt, despair, and resentment. At first, I was a little annoyed to have my thought pattern so abruptly broken, even if it was by the voice of the Lord! However, I quickly confessed my sinful attitude and accepted God's forgiveness. He then prompted me to praise Him regardless of the circumstances. I responded by praying forth in tongues, although the effort was admittedly somewhat less than vigorous.

Immediately I was challenged by the Devil. I was informed that my praise was both hollow and hypocritical. I was not praying from my heart at all, but merely mouthing syllables which were both mechanical and meaningless. The accusation so accurately matched my feelings that the only honest and reasonable thing to do was to stop praying at once. And, I did!

I am both amazed and thankful for the patient but persistent ministry of the Holy Spirit in His discipline of our lives. I had no sooner stopped praying than God began to deal with me in a stern but very positive way. The sequence of thoughts was somewhat as follows:

"My son, haven't I taught you certain principles from my Holy Word?"

"Yes, Lord," I replied.

"And, haven't I instructed you plainly that praying in tongues is not primarily a matter of feeling but of faith; and is not the time you need to pray the most the very time you feel like it the least?"

"Yes, Lord."

"Haven't I made it clear to you that when you are praying in the Spirit, you are permitting a heavenly expression which goes beyond the reason and understanding of your natural mind?"

"Yes, Lord."

"Haven't I specifically indicated to you that my Spirit will faithfully intercede for you when you don't even know how to pray as you ought?"

"Yes, Lord."

"And finally, didn't I warn you against measuring everything in terms of your blessing? Is not your prayer of faith well pleasing and a blessing to Me?"

"Yes, Lord."

"Then, my son, you must make up your mind. Are you going to put your faith and confidence in Me, my Word, my Son, and my Spirit, or in how you think and feel under the circumstances?"

I immediately told the Lord I was sorry; He was right and I had been wrong again. I asked for His forgiveness, and proceeded to forcefully pray in the Spirit without hesitation and without ceasing. There was no sense of overwhelming joy or happiness, only a sure sense of rightness. I continued for some time to pray as God had instructed me to do.

Then it happened! There was a knock on the door and the late arrivals suddenly made their appearance. Needless to say, at that moment I experienced a great deal of feeling and the meeting that followed was a most joyful occasion. Afterward, the Lord impressed me again concerning the power of prayer and praise. *Every answer begins in heaven in the realm of the Spirit before it is seen on earth in the realm of the natural!*

Sometimes the answer is not immediately forthcoming as in the example above, for such experiences are placed in our lives as lessons. *The man of faith, however, will persist in prayer and praise regardless of what the eye sees, the mind thinks, or the heart feels!*

"For everyone who keeps on asking, receives; and the one who keeps on seeking, finds; and to the one who keeps on knocking, the door will open" (Luke 11:10 Williams' translation). We, too, with Jesus, can simply but confidently confess, "Father, I thank You that You have heard me. Yes, I know You always hear and listen to Me" (John 11:41-42 *Amplified Bible*).

To be filled with the Spirit is to be filled with the power of unceasing prayer!

The Spirit and God's Word

"In the beginning was the Word and the Word was with God, and the Word was God . . . And the Word was made flesh, and dwelt among us, (and we beheld His glory, the glory as of the only begotten of the Father,) full of grace and truth" (John 1:1, 14).

The Greek word for "Word" in the New Testament passage above is "logos." It is a term which in its richest philosophical sense refers to a comprehension of concept, the totality of thought or an ideational reality which is fully expressed. *Jesus Christ is thus presented as the Divine Intention personified—the mind and heart of God realized in human form!*

He is the unique, personal, and living expression of God's love and wisdom in a manner which man can apprehend. In other words, Jesus is the "big idea" of what our Heavenly Father is really like in terms that we can understand, and to which we can warmly and personally relate.

The Holy Spirit Himself confirms the concept expressed above in the following passage from Scripture:

"Whereas in many parts and in many ways of old, God spoke to our forefathers in the words of the prophets, in this final age He has spoken to us in the person of His Son . . . Who is the outshining of His glory and the exact image and flawless expression of His very nature.

"For in Christ God gives a full and complete expression of Himself in human form" (Heb. 1:1-3, Col. 2:9 various translations).

What an exciting privilege it is to become better acquainted with God through the Lord Jesus as the Holy Spirit faithfully reveals to us the Person of the Living Word. It is the ministry of the Spirit to ever press us beyond the "letter" to the "Life" of God Himself. Very quickly we shall find that the Father's purpose in Jesus is the integrating theme throughout Holy Scripture. God's full will centers in His Son, and this truth is progressively revealed as one moves from Genesis to Revelation. We become an integral part of God's holy way when we become identified with His Spirit. *It is in God's Word that we discover the meaning of His will and way for our lives!*

One of the first things that newly Spirit-filled believers discover is that the Word of God has suddenly become alive for them in a new way. Many have been the times that we have been amazed at the fresh insights from God's Word that have been shared with us by college students who had recently come to know the fullness of the Holy Spirit in their lives. This should not be surprising, however, for as mentioned above, it is the purpose of the Holy Spirit to *illuminate* our understanding of God's Word (I Cor. 2).

It is most interesting when we become aware that the books of the New Testament were written by Spirit-filled believers to Spirit-filled believers. The authors of the Epistles took for granted that the recipients of their divinely inspired letters had already received both the gifts of God's Son and His Spirit. Pentecostal experience was the rule not the exception. A greater appreciation and understanding of the Scriptures are obtained when we realize that the grand themes of the Epistles find expression in our lives through the spiritual fruit and gifts. *The Word of God is the raw material the Holy Spirit uses to build Christ into our lives. As we live in the Word, the life of the Word becomes ours!*

The other morning I awoke with three words repeatedly going through my mind. They were these: informed, transformed, and conformed. As I pondered what significance the Holy Spirit would attach to this, the following thoughts began to develop. First of all, before we can become *conformed* into the image of Christ, we must willingly and faithfully expose our minds to His. The mind of God is revealed in His Word. Therefore, we must consistently expose ourselves to the Holy Scriptures. In this way we become Christ-*informed*. As we do, the Holy Spirit will *transform* and renew our minds like unto His (Rom. 12:2). We will progressively begin to think His thoughts rather than our thoughts. We will become more and more "Christ minded."

Now, our thoughts determine what we are, what we say and what we do. Therefore, to the extent that we think as Jesus thinks, we will be, say, and do as Jesus is, says, and does. In other words, we will become *conformed* into His image! How supremely important is God's Word for your life and mine!

How might one practically and personally begin to "search the Scriptures daily"? First of all, it is suggested that one obtain a standard Bible with large print and wide margins. A small plastic ruler and a micropoint ball pen will provide the means for underlining pertinent passages and personalizing them with marginal notes. A good concordance, Bible dictionary, and single-volume commentary are also recommended. To this should be added a modern version of the Bible for added accuracy and freshness. Spend some time in a Bible bookstore finding the volumes which are most readable and suited to your personal preferences.

One might begin with the Gospel of John and the Book of Acts and follow the events preceding and following Pentecost. Here are the reactions of people just like you and me as they entered into this new adventure of the Spirit-filled life. Try to imagine how you would have felt and acted if you had been there. *You will soon be reliving, in your life now, much of what you read in their lives then!*

Paul's Epistle to the Colossians is a beautiful and powerful portrayal of the preeminence and centrality of the Lord Jesus Christ. We see Him pictured as "Lord of all." We are "complete in Him," and now the Holy Spirit wants to increasingly make Him "complete in us." This is how He becomes Lord of our life!

The full beauty and power of Christ can only be found in the Church or body of believers. In Paul's letter to the Ephesians, we see the part we are to play in the ministry of the Church. The spiritual gifts and graces are the means of equipping our lives for the edification of the Church. We will have more to say concerning this in the next section.

Even in the Old Testament, spiritual truth will find expansion when it is recast into the words, works, and person of Christ. For example, the Psalmist declares that the godly man's "delight is in the law of the Lord; and in his law doth he meditate day and night" (Ps. 1:2). The Spirit-filled Christian would recognize the added significance this has for him when he realizes that the law is God's Word and that Jesus is the living Word and fulfillment of the law. To substitute Jesus for the word "law" lends a beauty to the passage which enhances our understanding. "The godly man's delight is in Jesus, and in Him doth he meditate day and night."

Sometimes it is meaningful to personalize spiritual *principles* and *promises* by restating the passage in the margin and inserting the pronoun "I" or "me." In this way, for instance, the spiritual principles in God's promises to Israel can become ours personally. Isaiah 43:1-2 declares: "Fear not: for I have redeemed thee, I have called thee by thy name; thou art mine. When thou passest through the waters, I will be with thee . . . How powerfully personal this becomes when in the margin we write, 'I am not to fear. Christ has redeemed me. I have been called by name. I am His. He is with me. I shall not be overwhelmed."

The Holy Spirit will always honor a positive confession of God's Word in faith. This is the means by which His will *for* our lives becomes real *in* our lives. The more we expose ourselves to God's Word, the greater becomes our faith in God's Word (Rom. 10:17). Through it the Holy Spirit brings peace and power and sustained purpose to our lives. Through the *written Word* the Holy Spirit imparts the *Living Word* to our lives. If we do not honor the place of the Holy Scriptures in our daily experience, we quickly grieve God's Spirit in us and frustrate His will for us. It is the deep desire of the Holy Spirit to make God's living Word our daily life. Jesus said, "I am the bread of life." May we quickly reply, "Give us this day our daily bread."

To be filled with the Spirit is to be filled with God's Holy Word!

3

The Spirit and Our Witness

The primary purpose of our Pentecostal experience is for power to witness to others of Jesus Christ. The word "witness" means to testify or furnish evidence of something we have seen, heard, or directly experienced. The Holy Spirit first makes Jesus Christ real to us in personal experience. He then enables us to furnish evidence of our living Lord to others by manifesting His life through us in thought, word, and deed. The fruit and gifts of the Spirit are the means by which others "see and hear" Christ in us. From this we can quickly see that the word "witness" means far more than passing out tracts or inviting someone to church, although on occasion both of these activities may be involved.

To live is to witness! It is not a matter of *whether* we are going to be a witness or not, but rather *what* we are going to be witnesses of and how effective that witness will be. The purpose of the Holy Spirit in our lives is that we may be a continual daily witness for Jesus Christ.

Witnessing for our Lord should be as real and natural as is our life. However, wherever, or whenever someone comes into our daily lives, he should encounter Jesus Christ. The rules for witnessing are basically very simple. *Live Christ and love others!* The way that love is expressed may be soft and gentle, or swift and powerful. Both expressions are found in principle and practice throughout the Epistles and the Book of Acts. The Holy Spirit sometimes moves powerfully as a mighty rushing wind, and oftentimes gently as a circling dove about to alight. Such, too, was the life of Christ. In gentle love He gathered the little children around Him. In great power He evidenced His authority by setting free those who were possessed by Satan's power.

There is no greater privilege given to man than that of sharing the Gifts of God's Son and His Spirit with others. As we give ourselves and each day back to God, may we pray that He will bring someone with a prepared and open heart across our path. May we be sufficiently sensitive to God and others to recognize the encounter when it comes. And, come they will, for *God will divinely order our lives to reach others if we expectantly ask Him to do so!*

Opportunities will surely come during the routine of our daily responsibilities. On other occasions we may wish to take the initiative ourselves and in a purposeful way go forth in faith and power to the "highways and hedges" beyond our usual lines of life.

Jesus urged us to pray that the Lord of the harvest would send more workers into the fields (Matt. 9:37-38). It is an honor to participate in such intercessory prayer, but even more wonderful to participate in the answer! It is as we aggressively go in faith that God will actually work with us and personally confirm His Word with the evidence of His saving and delivering power (Mark 16:15-20).

There are a variety of aids for witnessing which have been honored by God's Spirit in a most practical and personal way. Campus Crusade's "Four Spiritual Laws" (Arrowhead Springs, San Bernardino, California, 92403), and Billy Graham's "Do You Know the Steps to Peace with God?" (The Billy Graham Evangelistic Association, Box 779, Minneapolis, Minnesota, 55440), have been used in reaching thousands for Christ. These are little six-page leaflets that will assist an interested individual in making his personal confession of Jesus as his Savior.

The author has published a small forty-five-page booklet entitled *Life's Greatest Discovery,* which presents a witness for Christ from a scientific perspective. There are other materials available at any Bible bookstore. Ask God to help you become prepared for presenting Jesus to people in an effective and winsome way. Relate yourself to those in your Christian community who have discovered how to graciously share the Lord with others. They will be glad to encourage you to utilize the power of God's Spirit in this ministry of life.

Many times we may be only one link in the chain of love which God is forging to bring some lost sheep back into the fold. There are many ways of giving a cup of cold water to another in the name of Jesus. Just to smile at someone as Jesus would smile at them is one of the simplest ways to begin witnessing. To express a genuine interest in someone as a person will often pave the way by which we can introduce them to the most wonderful Person we have ever known. What a privilege to so share the Love and Life of God! I believe it was Rufus Moseley who on occasion would greet a stranger with the rather disarming remark, "God loves you and He told me to tell you so!"

It is the enemy that would stifle our witness by fear, coupled with a legalistic compulsion to duty. This is not God's Spirit of power or love and leads only to an awkward, strained situation.

I remember going to the barbershop once and trying in a forced way to think of some way to witness to the barber. I was feeling more and more distressed and condemned by my silence until finally the time was gone. (In my case, haircuts are never lengthy ordeals anyway.) As I was going out the door under a dark cloud of depression, the Lord simply said, "You could have talked to him about the weather in the name of Jesus!" I realized I had shown no interest in the gentleman, in even a personal, conversational way, so preoccupied had I been with my "duty."

In a subsequent visit, the Lord brought about a rather "natural" opportunity which allowed me to share rather freely concerning the love of God for people. It began with my discovery that I had left my sweater the last time I had been in the shop. The barber then related a story about an unclaimed coat that once had been left behind.

This reminded me of a friend of ours who had picked up a hitchhiker on a cold, rainy night while on a trip. The man had no coat and was obviously in financial distress. The Lord prompted my friend to offer him one of the two coats which he had brought with him in the car. Furthermore, God told him to give the hitchhiker the better coat. He finally obeyed and willingly offered the man his coat as an expression of God's love. With that the hitchhiker broke down and wept, confessing that he had fully intended to rob my friend before the trip was over. They both rejoiced in the personal way that God had expressed His grace.

I left the barbershop with the assurance that God had blessed my witness in a rather obvious way. In addition, the Lord impressed me with the difference between a forced, legal, loveless kind of testimony and the natural, gracious, lovely way in which the power of God's Spirit can go beyond the weaknesses of our own personalities.

We should continually be alert all through each day, for God may bring opportunities our way when and where we least expect them. Many times we have found ourselves sharing God's Word in situations we could never have anticipated. There is real adventure in the Christian life. God works in both marvelous and amazing ways to accomplish His will. If we ask God to prove Himself in our desire to be a Spirit-filled witness, He will take us at our word. You may find yourself in strange places sharing with strange people at strange times, but one thing is sure—you will never be bored. *The Holy Spirit is one sure cure for boredom!* Life will never be the same for the Spirit-filled believer. Every Christian should be motivated by this overwhelming sense of divine destiny.

When opportunities come to share God's Son and His Spirit with interested inquirers, let us be careful that *this* is what we share. We can tell them how God has confirmed His Word to us personally. We *know* God's Son! We *know* God's Spirit! It is our desire to introduce them to those whom we know and love. The best way to do this is to share how real God has made His Word to us in everyday life. We have to bring heaven to earth, for this is where they are.

This may involve time and patience. We reach over to others by the bridge of love. Jesus said, "Greater love hath no man than this, that a man lay down his life for his friends." What is our life? Is it not composed of our time, energy, interests, and desires? *Love will give life, ours for others!* As we so give of ourselves as He gave of Himself, there will come a time when the one whom God has loved through us will desire to enter into God's gifts. Our part then is to minister the Word of God in great faith and power. The Holy Spirit will always honor God's Word. This He will do regardless of time, place or circumstances! *Real faith will never limit God.*

A short time ago we visited some Spirit-filled Episcopalian friends in a nearby town. They told us of a young friend of theirs with whom they had shared their testimony. He was planning on entering the ministry and currently was employed as a television clown on a local children's program. The Sunday of our departure, our friends called and inquired if we would like to meet the young man. He had a television program in the afternoon and was going to the church afterward to perform for the children at an ice cream social. Following this, there were further commitments for the evening. There was the possibility, however, that we could visit with him for a little while between afternoon and evening commitments.

We arrived at the church social while he was in the midst of his performance with the children. Following this, he and my friend slipped away to the rector's study where we could visit together for a time. He removed his wig and sat down. He was still dressed in his clown suit and wearing makeup in colorful patterns. It was a strange combination of events that had brought us all together under such unusual circumstances.

We shared together of the Lord's leading in all of our lives, and of our mutual desire for His full will and power in each of us. I told him of the Holy Spirit's moving among Episcopalians we had known on the West Coast, and how our own lives had been changed by God's Spirit. We carefully related our experience to God's Word and God's Son. He warmly responded to all that we said and requested that we might pray with him that he, too, might know the fullness of the Holy Spirit in his life. As we all bowed our heads in worship, we prayed that God would honor the faith in his heart and fill him with an overflowing Spirit of praise. He immediately began to worship God in a heavenly language of love. Just as we were through, the door opened and his friend arrived to take him to his next appointment!

I couldn't help but think afterward of how marvelously the eternal God can divinely order the events of time to accomplish His purposes. Furthermore, we realized as never before that God is not limited by outward appearances or circumstances. *God will meet a searching soul anywhere or anytime his faith reaches out to embrace the promises of His Word.*

It is also comforting to know that God is not honoring us with all our limitations but the in-living Christ and His out-spoken Word. How wise it is for us to remember from time to time that we cannot convert anyone to Christ or fill anyone with God's Spirit. This is the work and responsibility of God alone. Our part is to show openhearted and ready-minded people how to exercise their faith in God's Word so they may receive God's gifts.

The scriptural pattern for active faith is simple and sure. "*Believe* in thine heart and *confess* with thy mouth." The greatest problem is convincing people from the Scripture that the pattern is really this simple . . . there is really nothing more to do; God has done everything else!

Our witness should always be very Christ-centered and firmly grounded in God's Word. Begin with Jesus and end with Jesus. Relate every experience to God's Word. God always confirms His Word in experience; therefore, the two must go hand-in-hand. Satan can cause us to doubt our experiences if we don't first find them firmly rooted in God's Word. Our experience will be only as strong as our faith is firm!

Many move into the Gifts of God's Son and His Spirit and then do not move on as they should because the purpose and support from the Scriptures is lacking. It is not enough to lead others into God's gifts alone. The meaning of the gifts must be grounded in the Word and related to God's purpose for their lives.

Just recently we visited for several hours with a Lutheran pastor on the Gulf Coast. It was one of those encounters which God brings into our lives for mutual profit. We shared our testimony with him and he shared with us. As his story unfolded, we learned that he had attended a meeting in the spring where an account of the Holy Spirit's move in the historic churches was given. He went to a side room for prayer and counsel afterward. He honestly told the Lord that he wanted anything God had for him, if through it he might better serve and worship God. Someone showed him the passage in Luke 11 which promises that if we ask we shall receive. He then in faith lifted his voice and spoke forth in a heavenly language of sustained praise as the infilling Spirit gave utterance. Some time later an elderly little lady approached him and indicated she had seen in a vision a white mantle which overshadowed him as he prayed.

In spite of such almost sensational experiences, he later began to question the validity of what had happened. In fact, he finally dismissed his experience as nothing more than autosuggestion. The Lord, however, over the next few months kept bringing the matter to his attention through his reading and contacts with ministerial colleagues. A seminary professor cautioned him about depreciating any gift God might give in response to a sincere prayer of faith based on God's Word and for His glory. He also discovered that one of his colleagues had just recently entered into the same experience in the Holy Spirit. Some of this had happened just prior to our visit with him. We then shared with him how God had meaningfully related our own personal experience in the Holy Spirit to His Word and to His Son.

We visited together for some time encouraging one another in the faith. As we parted, we both confessed God's utter faithfulness and our deep desire to worship and serve Him with every means that God's Spirit makes available to us. Devotional tongues was seen as a meaningful gift to edify us and glorify God. *True spiritual experiences will always appear both "right" and "real" when seen in the light of God's Word.*

Once again the Lord impressed upon me the necessity of grounding everything in His Holy Word. *God's Spirit will always honor God's Word to glorify God's Son.* Our experience is real because God's Word is real. The purpose of the Holy Spirit is to confirm the living Word of God in our lives. This is our witness!

To be filled with the Holy Spirit is to be filled with power to witness!

Fellowship in the Spirit

The Greek New Testament word for "fellowship" (koinonia) means sharing together in and around a common interest. The English words "communion," "community," and "communicate" are derived from the same root word. It was used in the marriage contracts of that day in reference to a life that was to be shared in common by the prospective partners.

When applied to Christian fellowship, the common interest around which we are united is a person. That person is Jesus Christ! Faith in Christ as our Lord and Savior will be the basis for our future fellowship together in heaven and should be the only basis for our Christian fellowship together here on earth. *The more real the love of Jesus becomes in and through our lives, the more real our fellowship with fellow believers becomes!*

We are born by God's Spirit into the Family of our Heavenly Father because of our life relationship with His Son and our Savior. Jesus has become our Elder Brother and we are therefore brothers and sisters to each other. We bear the same family name, and share the same glorious destiny, and are to express the same lovely life as that of our model Brother. We are united by the "life" we share in common with Him. This is the basis for a true and loving Christian community. Only an ecumenicity so born of the Spirit can ever be acceptable to our Heavenly Father.

One of the most striking and amazing characteristics of this latter-day outpouring of the Holy Spirit has been the bond of love for one another which marks real Spirit-filled believers. This Spirit of life cuts across all the barriers of peripheral doctrine and practice and links us together around Christ alone. *God has a way of mixing everybody up in His love when we submit to the harmonizing power of His Spirit.* Catholics, Episcopalians, Lutherans, Methodists, Baptists, Presbyterians, Nazarenes, Pentecostals, and a whole host of others are finding it really is possible to join together through the Holy Spirit as a Family that can sing, pray, worship, and work together for Jesus.

For so long we have fenced each other out of our respective fields of Christian endeavor. We have each played in our own little spiritual "puddles" but have cautiously guarded against contamination from another. The fences have been high and the wires sharply barbed. As the latter rain of God's Spirit began to be outpoured, the pools began to enlarge. To our initial dismay and amazement, the fields of some of our rivals were receiving the same refreshing rain that at one time we had exclusively claimed as our own. Furthermore, it was apparent the edges of the expanding pools were approaching our carefully constructed fences!

That was when we made a wonderful discovery: *Man-made fences cannot hold back the rising tide of God's Spirit!* In fact, as the water level rises heavenward, less and less of the fence posts can be seen. The separate pools have long since disappeared and there is an awareness that this move of God's Spirit may well "cover the whole earth as the waters cover the sea"!

Just before we laid hands upon a Catholic young man, who was a member of a scholastic order, for the Holy Spirit baptism, he requested that we first pray for the unity which Jesus had prayed we might have. He and another Catholic friend were very much interested in the power of the Spirit for their Christian service, but were aware of the many differences in the religious backgrounds of those of us who were sharing with them. What a privilege it was to confess the unity we had in Jesus as our Lord and Savior, and our desire to worship Him together. We had already sensed the bond of the Spirit which comes in genuine fellowship around the Lord Himself. We had gathered in His name, and He had drawn us unto Himself, and to each other. His love leaped all the earthly barriers which otherwise might have spoiled that holy hour.

Upon this ground of warm understanding, we prayed that the mighty Baptizer would fill our lives with the power of God's Holy

Spirit. Together, we submitted ourselves to His sanctifying presence. Together, we responded in faith to the infilling spirit of worship. Together, we magnified the Lord in heavenly tongues of praise!

Psalm 133 had become that day more than just a lofty ideal of some misty-eyed Old Testament poet; it was to us a genuine twentieth century reality! May this prophetic Psalm speak hope to all of our hearts as once again we carefully listen to its message of life:

"Behold, how good and how pleasant it is for brethren to dwell together in unity!

"It is like the precious ointment upon the head, that ran down upon the beard, even Aaron's beard: that went down to the skirts of his garments:

"As the dew of Hermon, and as the dew that descended upon the mountains of Zion: for there the Lord commanded blessing, even life for evermore."

Oil is a type of the Holy Spirit. Among other things, it speaks of spiritual healing and personal consecration. Zion represents God's chosen people. The morning dew symbolizes the promises and freshness of life which envelop the lives of God's people baptized by His Spirit. The fountainhead for such spiritual ministry is our Lord Himself, high and lifted up at the right hand of God. Aaron, the first high priest, anticipates the ministry of the Lord Jesus our Great High Priest who ever lives to make intercession for us. There is a sense in which He, too, like Aaron, received from His Father the anointing oil of consecration as He entered into His priestly ministry on our behalf after His ascension. The oil was likewise in abundant measure, for not only was His head anointed, but it descended downward in a mighty outpouring upon the many members which make up His earthly Body below (Acts 2:33). *What a revelation it is to realize that we all abide together in the same anointing as that of our Lord!*

One heavenly purpose for the Holy Spirit's power on earth is to unify and perfect Christ's Body, the Living Church. We are baptized into the Body of Christ when we are spiritually born into the family of our heavenly Father. *Any construction of man that separates true brothers and sisters of God's family from fellowship with each other inflicts a wound within the Body of Christ and is most grievous to the Holy Spirit.* Doctrinal and traditional distinctions are occasionally of serious importance and are not to be lightly glossed over; yet ultimately, they will not separate us from eternal fellowship together in heaven. Can we not anticipate such fellowship here on earth around the life of Jesus?

As we make this our glad confession and walk in the light of it, we

41

shall discover how good and how pleasant it is to dwell together in unity . . . for there we shall experience as a family the Father's promised blessing, even life—the altogether lovely and everlasting life of Jesus—for evermore!

We often sing with great feeling the little song, "We are one in the Spirit, we are one in the Lord . . . And they will know we are Christians by our love . . .!" It may be a little song, but it has a tremendous prophetic message. Jesus indicated that an important witness to the world that He truly was sent of God would be the unity of His followers (John 17:20-23). Here are His own words expressed in His intercessory prayer just prior to His crucifixion:

"I pray not only for these, but for those also who through their words will believe in me.

"May they all be one. Father, may they be one in us, as you are in me and I am in you, so that the world may believe it was you who sent me. I have given them the glory you gave to me, that they may be one as we are one.

"With me in them and you in me, may they be so completely one that the world will realize that it was you who sent me and that I have loved them as much as you loved me" (John 17:20-23 *The Jerusalem Bible*).

This unified witness of God's love for man (gospel) is to be worldwide in its scope and will usher in the coming of Jesus at His second advent. (Matt. 24:3, 14). The disunity, suspicion, and division within Christendom has prevented the world from seriously considering the claims of Christ. Even now, however, the Holy Spirit is bringing a healing to the whole Body of Christ which ultimately is going to produce a powerful, extensive testimony concerning the claims of God's Son. *The very weapon which Satan has used to weaken the witness of the church is going to become an instrument of truth which the world cannot ignore.*

Before it is all over, nobody will be able to use the excuse, "I never had an opportunity to really see the love and life of Jesus Christ in action." *There is going to be a glorious end-time witness of God's power through an anointed army of God's people!* All will be moving as one man under the leadership of Jehovah Sabbaoth (the Lord of Hosts). The Church will indeed become as an "army terrible with banners" against which the gates of hell shall not prevail.

How, in a practical and personal sense, do we as "living stones" find our place and purpose in this end-time expression of Christ's Church? To answer that question, let us move back through God's history book of the Church to its opening chapters. Here we can discover how the

Lord chose to shape the earthly material which was to hold His heavenly treasure as "His story" in time was to unfold.

A stream at its source is usually pure, even though in character it may not have the maturity which develops along the course of future events. There was indeed a clean simplicity to the character of the first Christian community as recorded by one who was on the scene when it all began. Luke, the historian, pictures for us the adventures of these heavenly pioneers during that precarious period of the past when the entirety of God's eternal purpose rested, humanly speaking, in their hands. I am sure all heaven watched with intense interest as the breath of God's Spirit fanned the newly set fires of conversion into leaping flames of life that soon were to be seen and felt "both in Jerusalem, and in all Judaea, and in Samaria and unto the uttermost part of the earth!" (Acts 1:8). Here is the story in Saint Luke's own words of how this remarkable fellowship was first started:

"When they heard this [Peter's Pentecostal sermon], they were cut to the quick, and they cried out to Peter and the other apostles, 'Men and fellow Jews, what shall we do now?' Peter told them, 'You must repent and every one of you must be baptized in the name of Jesus Christ, so that you may have your sins forgiven and receive the gift of the Holy Spirit . . .'

"Then those who welcomed his [Peter's] message were baptized, and on that day alone about three thousand souls were added to the number of disciples. They continued steadily learning the teaching of the apostles, and joined in their fellowship, in the breaking of bread, and in prayer.

"Everyone felt a deep sense of awe while many miracles and signs took place through the apostles. All the believers shared everything in common; they sold their possessions and goods and divided the proceeds among the fellowship according to individual need.

"Day after day they met by common consent in the Temple; they broke bread together in their homes, sharing meals with simple joy. They praised God continually and all the people respected them. Every day the Lord added to their number those who were finding salvation" (Acts 2:37-38; 41-47 Phillips translation).

From this account it is apparent that following water and Holy Spirit baptism, new converts were immediately introduced into the corporate life of the newly established Christian community. There they found and steadfastly maintained their place in the Lord.

It was a place of instruction, fellowship, and prayer. It was a place of power, praise, and holy wonder. It was a place of work, worship, and witness. It was a place of love, joy, and peace.

The community was characterized by God's love which is far more than a soft, sentimental feeling. It was evidenced by sacrifice and sharing; on occasion by kindly correction, or, if necessary, even firm discipline (Acts 5:1-11). It was the kind of love that was not blind to faults, but could keep on loving anyway. It was the oil of God's Spirit which kept the community sweet, even though the inevitable frictions of one life rubbing against another became evident (Acts 6:1). It was a ground from which the fruit of the Spirit could grow as "togetherness" became practical and real.

In his epistles, Paul defines some of the many ministries which the Lord Himself has personally and purposely placed within the Christian community:

"And His gifts were varied; He Himself appointed and gave men to us, some to be apostles, some prophets, some evangelists, some pastors and teachers . . . Others were given to us to be practical servants and assistants, personal sources of encouragement and exhortation, generous givers with sincerity, diligent leaders and administrators, 'glad angels of mercy' and miracle and wonder-workers" (Eph. 4:11; Rom. 12:6-8; I Cor. 12:28-29 various translations).

A "steadfastness" of character developed in the first Christian community as God prepared them for a time of persecution and dispersal which undoubtedly was inconceivable in the earlier days of their fellowship. God compressed much into their lives in those few short months of sharing together in His Spirit. Little did they know of the unexpected opportunities that soon would be forced upon them. But God knew! When the time of displacement came they were ready to "risk the glorious and reap the miraculous." And they did!

The following account is found in Acts 8:1-8 (*Living Gospels*):

"Saul was in complete agreement with the killing of Stephen. Beginning that day a great wave of persecution swept over the church in Jerusalem, and everyone except the apostles fled into Judea and Samaria . . .

"Saul was like a wild man, going everywhere to devastate the the believers, even entering private homes and dragging out men and women alike and jailing them. But the believers who had fled Jerusalem went everywhere preaching the Good News about Jesus!

"Philip, for instance, went to the city of Samaria and told the people there about Christ. Crowds listened intently to what he had to say, because of the miracles he did. Many evil spirits were cast out, screaming as they left their victims, and many who were paralyzed or lame were healed. So there was much joy in that city!"

Who knows how very important our community life in the Spirit may be in our day and age? How very little we, too, see of the future in any sure or predictable way. What a comfort it is to know God always prepares His people as they find their place in the fellowship of the faithful. What renewed interest becomes ours in recognizing the power and purpose God has placed in His holy Church. We will wish to pursue this further in both a practical and personal way.

The simplest expression of the Church is where two or three are gathered together in Jesus' name. He has promised to be there in the midst of them (Matt. 18:20). As we have seen, it is only through the Body of Christ or fellowship of believers that God's *full* glory can be manifested to the world. It is only through the fellowship of *many* believers that God's manifold expressions of beauty and power can be *fully* revealed. We each have an integral part of that power and beauty through the gifts and graces, but we need one another to make the divine picture complete. There are no free-lancers in God's economy! We all need the spiritual ministries of one another if we are to fulfill God's full will.

The new power which God desires to progressively release through the lives of Spirit-filled believers should be channeled back into one's local church! It is suggested that unless God leads otherwise, one should share his Pentecostal experience in the Holy Spirit with his pastor. Carefully explain how real Jesus Christ has become to your life and your deep desire to glorify Him in ways of Christian love. Assure your pastor, if he seems unduly concerned, that anytime he might feel it would be desirable, you will be happy to quietly withdraw in Christian love; but until then you feel your place is in the fellowship of the church. This will place a responsibility upon you to live a Christ-honoring life. It will also place the responsibility for any possible separation in fellowship upon others.

Real truth needs no defense; it will authenticate itself! One need never feel he has to defend himself or God. All we are required to do is to manifest Jesus Christ through our lives by His Spirit. We can always be ready to share the Gifts of God's Son and His Spirit with others as He provides the opportunity, but never is there any occasion for argument. This does not mean that there will not be opposition. The real test of brokenness before the Lord may come during times of unfair criticism and even persecution. Purpose in your heart to follow your Lord whatever the cost. There is no sweeter reward in all of life than to know you are in the center of His will, and God's will is Jesus, simply Jesus.

It is also imperative to find fellowship with other Spirit-filled believers if you are going to grow in the full purpose for which He has called you by His Spirit. As we have learned, there is the need to be further grounded in the Word as it is broken in Christian fellowship. You will also find that you have brothers and sisters who are going, or have gone, through the same valleys of possible doubts and discouragement which you may be facing. Furthermore, oftentimes our needs, whether physical or spiritual, may be met through the ministry of all the spiritual gifts (I Cor. 12:8-10). The very purpose of God's good gifts is to edify the Body and glorify the Head who is Jesus. You are an important part of the Body and in living union with the Head.

Also, as we grow in our spiritual life, we shall find God sovereignly prompting us to move out by faith into the exercise of some of the spiritual gifts. As your own ministry develops, you may find in God's grace that you are "excelling" more in some gifts than in others to the benefit of fellow believers. To learn and to grow with others is a mutually profitable experience.

Without Christian fellowship with Spirit-filled believers, all too often the faithless influence of others concerning the significance of His spiritual gifts will darken our sense of bright expectation. Once our faith is so dampened, the streams of God's Spirit in new and powerful ways will slacken, and we will find ourselves back in a "life as usual" sort of an existence. *Those who move in and "move on" nearly always are those who have continued to sharpen their newfound spiritual experience in warm Christian fellowship!*

We just have not been created to "go it alone"! A sustained lack of fellowship will almost always quench even the brightest flame of God's Spirit in a life. We need one another! God has admonished us in His Word to forsake not the assembling of ourselves together but to exhort and encourage one another all the more as we see the day approaching (Heb. 10:25).

Follow that prompting of God's Spirit for spiritual fellowship! Actually, Christian fellowship is the natural outcome and desire of an overflowing life in the Spirit. Go with an expectation of both sharing and receiving. Paul's pattern for a Spirit-filled meeting is that each participant should have a hymn, or a teaching, or a revelation, or an utterance in an unknown tongue, or an interpretation of it. "[But] let everything be constructive and edifying and for the good of all" (I Cor. 14:26, *Amplified Bible*).

We have experienced many times of fellowship in home prayer-and-share meetings that have followed this scriptural pattern. We have seen God's Spirit through His servants and by His gifts manifest God's Son in marvelous ways. There have been times of soul-searching and correction. There have been occasions of tenderness of God's Spirit sweetly moved across the hearts of sensitive believers. At other times, the whole group has joined in beautiful songs in the Spirit where both words and music were of a heavenly nature. Here is true worship in the beauty of holiness. Sometimes God would move powerfully and in spectacular ways to bring physical deliverance and healing. Perhaps after the ministry of God's Word, the Holy Spirit would bring meaningful confirmation to hearts and minds through prophecy or tongues and interpretation.

Often those who lack faith to receive the Holy Spirit in His fullness by themselves will find in the faith and wisdom of other Spirit-filled believers all the added encouragement that is needed. *Fellowship builds faith!*

The ways of God's choosing for meeting the needs of His people are unpredictable for any given meeting. His purpose, however, is always the same: to encourage, strengthen and quicken the believers, and magnify His Son—*to edify the Body and glorify the Head.* This is the fundamental principle for Christian fellowship of any kind. Every participant should be governed by this rule. The Holy Spirit will *always* honor with His manifest Presence *every* meeting that is so centered in God's Son. This is God's pattern for His people.

Real fellowship will follow through in real life. The consequence of sharing Jesus with fellow believers is a desire to also share Him with unbelievers. "That which we have seen and heard declare we unto you, that ye also may have fellowship with us: and truly our fellowship is with the Father, and with His Son Jesus Christ" (I John 1:3). The Body of Christ possesses *Life.* "Life begets Life!" Once we have experienced real *Life* there is an overwhelming desire to share it with others. Basically, that is what real spiritual fellowship is: the sharing of this *Life.* Jesus said, "I am . . . the life." Fellowship is simply sharing Jesus!

To be filled with the Spirit is to be filled with a desire to share the life of Jesus with one another!

5

The Spirit-filled Home

Six times over, God declared that His creation in the beginning was good in His sight. His seventh observation concludes with the startling statement that a situation existed which was not good in the light of His eternal purpose. "It is not good that man should dwell alone; I will make a help meet for him." *The desire of our heavenly Father has always been to have a family to and through which His life and love could be expressed.*

Eternal purpose had been born into the heart of Adam and in vain he sought for some expression in the beautiful array of living things which God had created that could complete his life—something that would relate to the unfulfilled sense of destiny which made him restless within. He had been created to share God's love with another and that someone was not to be found. We can almost feel the sense of sadness and personal disappointment which were Adam's in that early morning hour of creation when he faced the wonder of a whole new world . . . alone!

There is a touch of pathos climaxed with joy as one reads the record of the events which surrounded the very first marriage that God ever made:

"So the Lord God formed from the soil every kind of animal and bird, and brought them to the man to see what he would call them; and whatever he called them, that was their proper name. But still there was no proper helper for the man.

"Then the Lord God caused the man to fall into a deep sleep, and took one of his ribs and closed up the place from which He had removed it, and made the rib into a woman, and brought her to the man.

" 'This is it!' Adam exclaimed. 'She is a part of my own bone and flesh! Her name is woman because she was taken out of a man.' This explains why a man leaves his father and mother and is joined to his wife in such a way that the two become one person" (Gen. 2:19-24, *Living Books of Moses*).

God, Himself, established the first family in the history of mankind. Immediately, the Adversary appeared in an attempt to frustrate at the very outset God's plan for and through His people. The seed of death was sown in the heart of a man and Satan would have succeeded in a tragic timeless way if it had not been for another home, some thousands of years later, into which the Savior of the world was to come. And come He did! God is still going to have a people and His plan shall yet succeed. *Jesus is indeed the firstborn of a family of many sons and daughters all of whom will joyfully acknowledge God as their Heavenly Father and Jesus as their Elder Brother.*

Satan is a hard loser and still is striking at the home, both Christian and non-Christian, in a frantic display of his wrath as he sees his final hour approaching. The family unit represents the simplest expression of the living Church in action! Jesus said that where two or three are gathered together in His name there He would be to honor our confessions of faith to our Father (Matt. 18:18-20).

The Enemy especially recognizes the power and authority which the Spirit-filled home can generate, and He does not remain idle in view of this. It is encouraging that wherever the Adversary comes in like a flood, God has promised to raise up a standard against him (Isa. 59:19). This is precisely the picture which we have found at the level of the home and family wherever we have gone in our ministry for the Lord. Many lessons have been learned and God has repeatedly emphasized the importance of the truth which we shall shortly share together. All of it has been born out of experience and relates in a most practical way to one of the most important centers of both spiritual conflict and promised blessing.

Basically, the relationship of marriage and the family is one of sharing together in life. In God's divine order, this begins at the level of our life in Christ. It is only as a husband and wife become spiritually alive together in Him that God's full purpose can be achieved through their lives as He intended. Consequently, the Apostle Paul gets a running start on his discussion concerning the Christian home by first encouraging the Ephesian believers to ever be filled to overflowing with the Holy Spirit. He then identifies some of these streams as the rivers of praise, joy, and thanksgiving. The last stream he considers is one which is not often emphasized among the fruit of the Spirit. *It is the stream of mutual submission!* (Eph. 5:18-21).

There is a spiritual principle behind our learning to submit to and thereby share the life of Jesus in and with each other. It is the cornerstone of truth upon which God is going to build His Triumphant Church! The greater is usually gained at the level of the lesser. It is as we learn to live together with each other at the level of the home that we will learn to witness and worship together as members of God's greater family. The everyday life and problems of the home become the earthly ground from which the fruit of the Spirit can most effectively grow. The Holy Spirit is a very practical person who desires to bring practical answers to practical problems. Let us see how this works out in real life.

We will wish to consider first of all some of the practical aspects that relate to a home where all members are filled with the Spirit and desire to move on with God. We also will want to face situations which are less than ideal; where one or more members don't really know Jesus as the Savior, or, if they do, are disinterested or antagonistic to some aspects of Holy Spirit baptism.

Let us begin by considering some simple but basic concepts concerning the various phases of ministry which are related to a Christian marriage. Throughout our entire discussion we will be interested in spiritual principles which will minister life. To fall into a legal attitude will only bring frustration and eventually death, spiritually speaking. The words that God would speak to us are Spirit and they are life! (John 6:63).

THE THREEFOLD MINISTRY OF THE
SPIRIT-FILLED HUSBAND AND WIFE

There is a threefold spiritual ministry which God has ordained for every Christian couple. *The first area of ministry is to each other in mutual edification and encouragement.* This involves praying and

51

sharing together in God's Word. This is a very practical way of keeping communication lines clear at other levels. The Lord holds our unity in His Spirit as supremely important.

The second area involves their ministry together as parents within the home, and also their witness as a couple to the world without. Jesus teamed His disciples in twos and then sent them forth with the authority of His name. There are some things a man and wife (and father and mother) can accomplish as a team which could be achieved in no other way.

The third area of ministry involves that which is personally unique. A wife and mother has spiritual responsibilities and privileges which are distinctively and specifically hers. This same is true of a husband and father. Again, this will involve opportunities both inside and outside the home situation. Every person has a particular place and a divinely-ordained function in the Body of Christ which never should be depreciated or suppressed.

The distinct character of the threefold ministries is to be recognized and appreciated by both marriage partners. It is their privilege to encourage each other to excel in the gifts and graces which will enable them to express the life of Jesus in all of these areas of spiritual responsibliity. As we shall see, where these three ministries are not appreciated and related to each other, serious problems can arise.

SHARING TOGETHER IN THE LIFE OF JESUS

Before considering the specific roles of husband and wife in the Christian home, it would be well to consider the unity of spirit and harmony of heart which can be achieved only as we learn to share together in the life of Jesus. God desires that our communication with Him and with each other be carefully guarded as something that is most precious in His sight. An openness in love is the best remedy for hidden, festering resentments. Something as simple as daily devotions *together* can help us keep short accounts with each other and the Lord if Jesus is truly welcome in our midst. It is difficult to hold a hurt or a grudge in our heart and pray in the Spirit together at the same time. *The convicting power of the Holy Spirit will consistently crowd us to the cross for forgiveness!*

The Lord taught my wife and me the significance of sharing together in Jesus even before we were married. The Holy Spirit is a marvelous marriage-maker, and, I discovered, a very clever and effective cupid. We both, unknown to each other, had arrived at a point of commitment to Christ which involved God's will in every area of our lives.

One Sunday afternoon in my dormitory room at Rice University, where I was taking my graduate training, I prayed that I might find a companion who was going the same way with God—as I had recently found Him—that we might go with Him together. My future wife had recently discovered the Lord in a new and personal way and had likewise submitted to His will concerning the possibility of marriage and a Christian home. To shorten the story, for the Lord had several hurdles in the natural to overcome (one of which was my timidity), we found each other that very night after the evening church service. It was a rather rapid and remarkable answer to prayer. That was in the fall; the following June we were married!

As mentioned above, God began to teach us the significance of sharing together in Him. Before our marriage, I would call her every evening, and then, upon returning to my room, would have my time of devotions. At the same time she was also reading and praying, so we sensed a togetherness in our worship with the Lord. Consequently, it was the most natural thing from the very first day of our marriage to continue our daily devotions together and to honor His presence in the usual problems and concerns of early homemaking.

The years have now passed and our prayer together goes beyond just the "devotional time," and involves the Lord in our conversation anytime we feel the need and desire to recognize and confess His wisdom and power. We often pray as we travel along the freeways, allowing God to make the car a holy altar on wheels. *Any place is holy where Jesus is!* This may seem to be a rather simple theme, but I have discovered in counseling with many who are facing marriage problems, that sharing together with Jesus in prayer is a missing dimension in their home. It can also be the beginning of a genuine healing in their lives.

Harmony in the home is based upon a unity of the Spirit which brings a oneness of heart and mind. God places a supreme value upon our "togetherness" in Him. Some years ago, when the Holy Spirit was freshly moving among the historic churches on the West Coast, the Lord taught my wife and me an important lesson concerning our unity in the Spirit. I had been going to meetings of all sorts, even on short notice, as if God's entire plan of the ages rested upon my shoulders alone. My wife had been very patient and understanding concerning my great zeal in the Lord, even though on some occasions my decision to go somewhere was more in terms of an announcement than it was a matter of mutual prayer and agreement.

It all came to a crisis one evening when I cautiously informed my wife of another important meeting which I felt it necessary to support with my presence. I could tell from the back of her head the idea hadn't set too well, but since a visiting student was helping her do the dinner dishes, she didn't voice her contrary feelings. I took advantage of the opportunity and slipped away, confessing bravely to the Lord that even though family and friends might misunderstand, still I would be true to "my ministry" for His kingdom. The meeting wasn't as important as I had thought it would be, but one never knows when God might break through in some spectacular way, and if He did, I was pretty sure He would want my help!

When I arrived home, my wife was more distressed than I had ever seen her in all our married life. I realized I had not taken her concern and feelings as seriously as I would have, had I been more sensitive to God's Spirit. The Lord was faithful in the midst of it all, however, and impressed us to rest in Him for the night and discuss the situation together in the morning. We also sensed there was something about which He wished to deal with us.

After breakfast the next day we submitted ourselves to the Lord and to each other with open and humble hearts. I realized my zeal for God had assumed a strong, striving spirit which had pushed me into the area of pride. My wife recognized that her resentment had not been brought to the cross for His inner work of redeeming grace. But, more than this, God, Himself, revealed His mind to us concerning the basic problem.

We were assured that in times of disagreement, His primary concern was not with who was right or wrong, but rather with why our unity in His Spirit had been broken. The next order of the day was not the decision we had considered so important, but a restoration of our communion in Christ. Sometimes this would mean giving up our respective positions to the Lord, realizing He would return to us *both* whatever was truly His will and pleasure; there might even be an alternative which the Holy Spirit was waiting to reveal.

Such mutual submission to Jesus and each other is not always easy when everything natural within our lives is geared for conflict. But the baptizing power of Jesus can release us from ourselves, if we are willing and obedient. There is no sweeter victory in all the world than to see Satan yield to the authority which God has invested in those who purpose to dwell together in unity through the power of His Spirit. My wife and I have subsequently had many opportunities to prove the wisdom of God's instruction for us. We both can confess with real conviction, based on experience, that the working power of the Holy Spirit is most effective in very practical ways!

THE ROLE OF THE SPIRIT-FILLED HUSBAND

"For the husband is the head of the wife, even as Christ is the head of the church . . . Husbands love your wives, even as Christ also loved the church, and gave himself for it; That He might sanctify and cleanse it . . . [and] present it to himself a glorious church, not having spot, or wrinkle, or any such thing" (Eph. 5:23, 25-27).

"Husbands, live with your wives with understanding and consideration, honoring them as the weaker vessel, and as being heirs together, sharing in the grace of life; that your prayers may not be hindered" (I Pet. 3:7 various translations).

These and other Scriptures make it very clear that God has given a priestly ministry to the husband as the head of the home. The Lord holds him primarily responsible for the spiritual welfare of the family. With this responsibility the Lord provides both divine authority and power to graciously fulfill every related obligation. This would be impossible apart from the gifts and graces of the Holy Spirit which lift us beyond our natural limitations.

The husband is not only responsible before the Lord to excel in his own unique ministry in the family of God, but he is to appreciate and encourage the personal ministry which belongs to his wife. This would involve reassurance, on some occasions, protection, and even spiritual counsel, should such direction appear advisable. Never is his authority to be harsh or heavy-handed, but rather a blessing as is the Lordship of Jesus.

I asked a very successful businessman who was really the spiritual leader in his home. After some hesitation, he confessed he had relegated this role to his wife, who, besides being a very strong personality, was a very gifted woman with an outstanding ministry in the Spirit. He explained further that she spent hours in prayer and study, and his business obligations prevented him from delving as deeply as she did into spiritual things. Consequently, he had yielded this responsibility to her. He had rationalized his role as merely providing for her material welfare and thereby supporting her ministry for the Lord.

Sadly, he had failed to realize that the God of eternity does not always measure spirituality in terms of clock hours. Furthermore, God always provides the spiritual gifts necessary for his divinely appointed responsibilities. The spiritual disorder in their home was reflected in other members of their family who, likewise, had submitted to a definite, dominating influence that characterized her life. Some of the scars were painfully deep.

Strong spiritual ministries of women which overshadow the authority of their husbands in the home have a tendency to influence other women in a similar way. To willfully ignore divinely instituted leadership can lead only to disorder and limitation in God's greater family as well. How very much the loving authority and guiding wisdom of this husband was needed in his home! What a greater blessing his wife could have been in the body of Christ if he had accepted his God-given priestly ministry for the family. One also wonders if there wasn't a latent ministry which was uniquely his that has remained undeveloped because somewhere along the line business interests were substituted for spiritual responsibility!

Some husbands, on the other hand, assume a position of rightful authority, but without the tenderness that characterizes the Christlike life. It is possible for even gifted men of God to be less than gracious in the home. I have seen husbands humiliate their wives in front of others by depreciating remarks which were devastating in effect. Jesus did not come to destroy, but to heal and make people whole. *Love is kind and courteous!*

One should never exert a dominating influence upon the life of another to the extent that he no longer feels worthwhile as an individual. It is a serious thing to suppress the soul of those whom God desires to free. The baptizing power of Jesus should bring a glorious release in the Spirit to every member in the home in very practical ways. Being "heirs together in the grace of life" involves time as well as eternity. How beautiful it is when a husband and wife respect each other and together make decisions in the Lord concerning such practical things as family finances and thereby bring a heavenly quality to earthly affairs!

"Christ so loved the church that He gave Himself for her . . ." There is another dimension to the love of a truly Spirit-filled husband for his wife if it is truly to be Christlike in quality. It involves a willingness to be first in submitting to the cross of self-denial when it is necessary to bridge the communication gap that disagreement can bring. "Communion" and "communication" come from the same Greek root word, which also includes the concept of fellowship.

When the spiritual fellowship is broken between a man and his wife, there is also a breach in their communion with the Lord. This is a grievous wound to the body of Christ and only the unifying ministry of the cross can heal the stripe so carelessly inflicted upon His back. *Usually we are so concerned about our own hurt feelings that we fail to think of the pain this brings to the Lord!* No wonder the Scriptures speak of the Spirit as being grieved by such behavior (Eph. 4:30—note the context!).

When personal disagreements develop to the point that our communion in the Spirit is spoiled and a stubborn stalemate is the result, only the cross can restore our fellowship in the Lord. Furthermore, as the head of the home, God expects the husband in Christlike love to go to the cross first! This is easier said than done, but the purpose of the Holy Spirit is to give to us the power to do a right thing whether we feel like it or not.

"Going to the cross" means dying to our pride and self-pity and apologizing for a spoiled attitude of heart and mind. The inner approval of the Holy Spirit will come *after* we make our decision and as we follow through, not before. An attitude of humility in one heart will tend to reproduce itself in the life of another, and then the problem, which was as inflated as our egos, likewise collapses to its realistic size. Now God's word of wisdom can find the spiritual soil necessary for its reception and solution-producing life. (As the reader probably has already assumed, the author is writing from some rather practical, personal experiences. Again, one can say most emphatically—it really does work! I must admit, however, that on some occasions my wife has outraced me to the cross. The important thing is that we both finally arrived!)

THE ROLE OF THE SPIRIT-FILLED WIFE

"And the Lord God said, It is not good that man should be alone; I will make him an help meet for him" (Gen. 2:18).

"Wives, submit yourselves unto your own husbands, as unto the Lord" (Eph. 5:22).

"See to it that you deeply respect your husband—obeying, praising and honoring him; and deferring to him and loving and admiring him exceedingly" (Eph. 5:33 various translations).

As the husband assumes his role, it will not be difficult for the Spirit-filled wife to accept with appreciation her role as clearly outlined in the Scriptures above. A husband cannot truly be the whole man God intended for him to be apart from his wife. Likewise, a wife actually cannot find and fulfill her own life apart from the ministry of her husband. She will discover her real destiny as divinely ordained only as she submits to the headship of her husband in the home.

Strong-souled women who usurp the spiritual leadership in the family will ultimately reap great limitation in terms of God's holy purposes! Such situations often develop where the wife is filled with the Spirit first and then moves rapidly into revelation, prophecy, and other gifts. The husband is directly or indirectly shamed for not keeping pace with his wife and consequently either submits to her seeming spiritual superiority, or shuns the whole scene and endeavors to salvage his ego by excelling in some secular activity such as his business.

Very often wives in similar situations gravitate to each other and develop strong, dominating ministries which can isolate other wives from their husbands as well. Often such meetings become mystical and are prone to error. There is an emphasis on special revelations which lead to self-exaltation and isolation from the body of Christ as a whole. (Although there may be an emphasis on Jesus in a mystical sense, it is in a way which relieves them from any practical control outside the privileged group.) Usually individuals so involved are most unsubmissive to even kindly correction and justify their position on the basis of having pressed through to "deeper truth" which cannot be fully appreciated by those "less sensitive" to the Spirit.

Such deviations from wholesome Christian fellowship are not limited to women's groups by any means, but the latter are perhaps particularly prone to such deception, if those involved willfully ignore the principles of spiritual leadership in their own home. Had Eve submitted to the headship of Adam and patiently waited, until together they could discern the truth concerning the first temptation, the story might have ended quite differently! The Apostle Paul indicates it wasn't Adam who was deceived (not that he was immune), but rather Eve who was deluded and fell into sin (I Tim. 2:14).

Sensitivity to the Spirit-world, coupled with a rather emotional nature, needs the balance of that stability which wisdom and God-given understanding can bring. The latter ministries of the Spirit are not as sensational or spectacular as some of the other gifts, but are absolutely necessary to maintain a straight path. *How very much we need each other in the body of Christ!*

The author in his travels across the nation has seen the tragic results which follow the temptation to be free from all spiritual restraint, which God's divine order for the home wisely and graciously provides. The danger cannot be overemphasized, but must be seen in the safety of the Lord's divine plan.

A lady was determined to visit a noted healing evangelist, for she was convinced through special revelation that she, too, was gifted. It became my responsibility to respond to her questions in a personal interview. Her husband came with her, but was very mild and soft-spoken. She answered most of the questions which I directed toward him. We soon centered our conversation around Jesus, however, and they both warmly responded, and we became better acquainted. The picture soon became clear. Her claims to revelations and special gifts had elevated her to a place of spiritual leadership in the home. Emotionally, she was not capable of handling the responsibilities involved. Finally, I spoke rather forthrightly, explaining to her how much she really needed her husband's quiet counsel and stability. She was so tense I wasn't sure how much was actually registering, but her husband seemed to respond.

After a time, it became apparent that neither had been baptized by Jesus in the full sense of the experience. Both expressed a desire for all God wanted for them and requested prayer. I indicated I first would pray with her husband, since he was to be the priest in their home. He immediately and restfully responded with a most fluent expression of heavenly praise in tongues. The peace on his face spoke of a simple, relaxed relationship with Jesus which their home desperately required.

We then prayed for her, but she wasn't able to find a full release in the Lord, so intent had she been in her previous struggle for recognition. Hopefully, her husband assumed his rightful role in the days that followed and encouraged her desire to serve the Lord in a more restful and gracious way. His ministry to her was more needed than either of them realized.

On another occasion, my wife invited a visiting student to share with me a spiritual concern which they had discussed, involving her former experiences. She was in her middle twenties and had recently been released by the Lord from a rather unpleasant past. She had been accepted into a Christian home along with several other girls with the purpose of getting stabilized in their newfound life in Christ. Two gifted women had established the ministry as a means of encouraging young ladies who needed to be grounded in God before assuming the responsibility of facing the world on their own.

Both of the women in charge were greatly gifted along the lines of revelation, prophecy, and deliverance. What began so graciously, however, became a source of great spiritual distress. The atmosphere of love and kindness could become harsh and psychologically cruel if either of the two women was crossed. The "gifts" were used to establish their authority, and anyone who refused to submit was directly or indirectly threatened with divine punishment!

The student had left, in spite of warnings that she was out of the Lord's will and would suffer God's judgment. It was with fear that she went, but once apart from the dark and dominating influence of the two women, she was reassured by the peace of the Lord. I inquired about the husbands of the women, and, as might be anticipated, neither of them was the spiritual leader of his home. Once again, we saw a meaningful ministry which had drifted into error because God's divine order for the family had been ignored.

There are beautiful and lovely stories to share as well, for the Holy Spirit will honor God's Word in most marvelous ways when we accept its principles for our own lives. The following testimony was written by a wife and mother in the Midwest who decided to hold to God's principles and claim His promises:

"After receiving the Baptism of the Holy Spirit, my one desire was that my family would also share this dimension of reality, and that we truly be one in the Spirit. For me, it had to be more than just the testimony of my words. I wanted them to see something in my life that they wanted!

"The desire to 'give every man a reason for the hope that was within me' drove me to the Word, for this is what He promises to watch over and perform. When the Enemy sought to divide or make me think I must press ahead alone, the Holy Spirit would remind me, 'Of one flesh hath He made you, called according to His purposes.' I also saw in the Word that the husband is head of the wife, so I sought God to bring Paul (my husband) forth as the spiritual head of the household . . . That winter he joined a study group on the Holy Spirit and subsequently received the Baptism himself at a service where Harald Bredesen ministered.

"As the Lord caused me to accept leadership in Bible studies and prayer groups, He also has quietly reminded me in regard to my husband, 'He must increase, and I must decrease,' even as with my Lord. How faithful He has been! First, He gave my husband a sixth-grade Sunday School class to teach and with which to grow. Paul then started a noon Bible study at his office which has prospered for three years, and has given a real outlet for sharing. In the evening groups, we all share together and each has something to contribute which no other can . . .

"It is so very practical to recognize that nothing just happens; that our steps are ordered of the Lord. Consequently, we look for His purpose in everything! God provided us with a mountain home, but we were led to finish the interior ourselves. As a result unsaved men from my husband's office have graciously offered help, along with our Spirit-filled friends and we have observed the Holy Spirit drawing them to Jesus and ministering to all in a natural, spontaneous way."

Another lady, who was greatly used in a teaching ministry to women, extended her faith to claim her unsaved husband as the head of her home. She never accepted a speaking engagement unless he was agreeable. Her requests were reasonable and he never refused. One evening, however, he did express his preference for her to remain at home. At first she stiffened in resentment, but quickly reaffirmed her commitment to honor her husband's desires in this area as from the Lord. To her consolation, she later learned, the nature of the meeting would have placed her in a very unpleasant and embarrassing position. How grateful she was that God had chosen this means of both sparing her personal discomfort and simultaneously confirming her commitment!

To claim one's mate by faith as *already* in God's chosen place of responsibility and wherever possible, as prompted by the Spirit, to seek his counsel and advice will often help maintain a restful atmosphere in the home. If we strive in a soulish way to move our mates to the Lord, either as Savior or Baptizer, we shall only succeed in hindering the pursuing power of the Holy Spirit. I recall a wife who, in a spirit of disappointment almost bordering on disdain, described how far short her husband was from her ideal of a spiritual leader. One could almost detect a little bit of pride in her impatience. None of these qualities speak of the winsome graces that can attract a person to the Lord. I suggested that instead of continually confessing what was wrong with her husband, she should see him as God desires him to become and wherever possible begin responding to him as the head of the house.

If we don't see by faith our loved ones in the healing hands of Jesus, we will start pushing them around with our own! I did this with my wife in regard to the baptism in the Holy Spirit. We had been moving together in our walk with the Lord until I was filled with the Spirit as described earlier. I then began to pressure her psychologically to attend all kinds of meetings, so she, too, might meet the "gentle dove" of God's Spirit. She reacted so emphatically that after a couple of weeks I gave up in sheer despair.

The day she did receive her baptism in the Holy Spirit, I recall telling someone how blue and discouraged I was. I finally had concluded that if she was ever going to be filled with the Holy Spirit, God was going to have to do it! I had decided I was going to take my hands off completely and leave the matter totally up to the Lord. That night she voluntarily suggested we go to a home prayer meeting where a man mightily used of God was going to speak. The whole evening was practically dead until shortly before 10:00 p.m. The Spirit of God then moved in prophecy indicating His desire that we seek His face in prayer. With great expectation, everyone headed for a place to pray.

We had a newborn baby just a few weeks old, and about 10:00 p.m. my wife always became restless and wanted to return home. I would usually try to pressure her to stay at the meetings a little longer. This evening, however, as much as I wanted to stay for her sake, I decided I was really going to keep my commitment to God not to interfere. I even went so far as to approach her first to suggest perhaps we might want to go home to the baby. I was about to speak when she went by me like I wasn't there—heading for a green sofa on the other side of the room.

She knelt and immediately began to pray that God would fill her with His Holy Spirit. I felt I didn't have to hold back any longer, and I remember I fell all over myself getting the visiting evangelist to her side. I was so excited he couldn't understand me at first. Needless to say, this was all God had been waiting for . . . for me to get out of the way! She was beautifully baptized in the Holy Spirit to our mutual joy that very hour.

My wife has ministered encouragement to me in many more ways than I can tell. There are times when her discernment has been more sensitive than mine, and we are learning to carefully listen to God's voice together. She has a disarming way of quoting my own words when God is prompting me to practice what I preach! I can personally testify that one of the most precious gifts the Lord can give a man is companion with whom the wonderful adventure of the Spirit-filled life can be shared.

THE ROLES OF SPIRIT-FILLED PARENTS AND CHILDREN

"Fathers, do not rouse your children to resentment, but rear them tenderly in the training, discipline and counsel of the Lord" (Eph. 6:4 various translations).

"Children, obey your parents in the Lord: for this is right. Honour thy father and thy mother; which is the first commandment with promise; that it may be well with thee, and thou mayest live long on the earth" (Eph. 6:1-3).

The Lord impressed me once that I was to be as patient and long-suffering with my children as He was with me! The love of God is neither blind nor sentimental. It often involves both discipline and direction, but within the context of faith, hope, and understanding. Divine love is powerfully persistent, yet graciously tempered with tender mercy and humility (I Cor. 13:4-7; I Pet. 3:8-9).

It takes the power of the Holy Spirit Himself to translate such a lofty ideal into an earthly reality. Once again we appreciate the admonition of the Apostle Paul, that we ever be filled with the Holy Spirit. There is no alternative by which a heavenly harmony can come to our homes. Where else might there be a greater need in a very practical way for the power which only the fruit and gifts of the Spirit can bring?

As our own children entered into their teenage years, many of the usual problems of communication and understanding began to develop. I have learned many life principles concerning my own relationship with my heavenly Father and other members of His family through experiences with my own family. Often the discipline of His hand rested heavily upon me as I would seek to solve family problems (all of which have spiritual centers) in a strong, self-willed way.

God dealt with me in my need to trust both my children and His Spirit concerning the temptations which every teenager must face. There is a sense in which it is better to have trusted our children and have been disappointed for a time than not to have trusted them when we should have. This does not mean we can be careless or unconcerned about our responsibilities relative to their companions and activities. But, God would have us stand with Him in a strong faith concerning His keeping and protecting power. *The Lord once reproved me for always picturing my children in the hands of the Devil, rather than in the hands of Jesus!* My faithless attitude resulted in harsh and heavy-handed endeavors to line out their lives without the courtesy of including their feelings in my decisions. I forced my will, but lost their love and respect!

The Lord in His grace began to show me the importance of recognizing their growing need to become individuals whose spiritual dignity was to be respected. Their responsibility to God was becoming something direct and personal, rather than secondhand relationship through their parents. This meant giving them enough freedom, within defined limits, to make mistakes while still within a family environment of redeeming love.

The shifting of our confidence from natural parental discipline to that of the Spirit for the children involved some painful episodes. I, especially, was slow to completely trust God's work in their lives and repeatedly interfered with my own endeavors which were often motivated by a strong, proud spirit. There were even times, if I felt I was not eliciting the quality of repentance I felt was appropriate, when I threatened them with God's hand of judgment! More than once the Holy Spirit so severely convicted me of my un-Christlike attitude and actions, that I was required to apologize for facing a problem with them in a way that had displeased God.

It is so easy in the interaction of personalities for one wrong attitude to elicit a corresponding spirit in a negative reenforcing cycle. Such downward spirals can be stopped only by someone responding to the releasing power of the Holy Spirit and thereby breaking the vicious circle. God impressed me quite specifically along these lines when our boy was younger than he is now. He had pushed one of his sisters for some minor annoyance which so often assumes gigantic proportions in the eyes of those involved. I reprimanded him rather severely for striking back at his sister in such an ungentlemanly fashion. He flared up and violently informed the whole household that he hated his sisters' irritating ways and wished they were dead! Whereupon I reacted as violently as he had and the matter developed into a rather superheated situation.

After the smoke cleared away and nothing was left but the ashes of what might have been a wonderful testimony of God's grace, the Lord began to speak to my heart. I was informed that I had reacted to a circumstance rather than responding to His redeeming Spirit. As a father, not only had I failed to lift my son up to a level of greater maturity, but had fallen to his level of immaturity and lost an opportunity for the fruit and gifts of the Spirit to be translated from theory to practice.

The Lord then instructed me as to how I should have responded in firm but gentle wisdom. How much better it would have been to have explained to my boy that there are times when everybody wishes they could get away from it all, especially people! However, life involves people and we can't always escape from irritating situations. This is the raw material of life which God can use to make us more mature in our responses to unpleasant situations. *In one sense the family is the testing and proving ground for life as it will be lived at all of its other levels!*

The next time a similar circumstance arose, rather than submitting to a hasty spirit of reaction, I allowed the Holy Spirit to first discipline my own life and then quietly shared the words the Lord had previously given. To our full satisfaction, we saw the Lord actually redeem the explosive situation, not only for our personal insight and edification, but for His own glory and pleasure as well! There is something very gratifying in seeing God perform His Holy Words in the power of the Spirit just when we need it the most.

Another area the Lord loosened up for more of His life was our time for family devotions. The children had been reared to participate in Bible reading and prayer from the very beginning of their lives. As they approached and entered their teens. I became more legal in enforcing their respect for God's Word and prayer. This, of course, resulted in a reaction to me rather than a response in their hearts to God.

The Lord impressed us that He was more concerned about their hearts being open than some artificial issue about how distracting the presence of the cat might be. Where I used to discourage any discussion other than that which directly pertained to our Scripture reading, now we enjoy a family time that can involve all of the interests or concerns of the day. God's Word and prayer in one sense is supposed to be mixed in with every part of our lives. Too often we make a false distinction between the sacred and the secular, that in effect restricts God to a rather narrow segment of our life experience. *Sometimes we don't realize how spiritually uptight we are until the Holy Spirit sets us free!*

At the time of this writing, we are all still in the process of learning together all that God wants for our home. But we are finding that faith in Jesus and each other is a very satisfying way to live. The Lord is still forcing hidden things to the surface of all our lives for His releasing touch, but He has assured us that His hand of love will never fail, if we purpose to follow Him in faith and obedience. As we have become more restful within our lives, the children have responded in a way which has increasingly brought the joy of the Lord to our home. It is wonderful to really enjoy each other in Jesus!

The principles outlined above have been proven in the homes of many Spirit-filled families across the nation. I know a family in the Midwest who had two wayward children on drugs; yet, they stood firm in their faith in God and love for the youngsters. They accepted them back into their home upon their return and steadfastly claimed their full release unto Jesus. God gave them the power and wisdom to go victoriously through some trying days as He worked in hidden, inward ways to reclaim two wayward children to Himself.

God impressed me during the entire time that everything was in spiritual order in the family, even though outwardly the situation was far from ideal. God recognizes hearts of faith and sees as complete that which yet requires time in the natural. Consequently, their home was a source of life in many ways to the Christian community.

They not only maintained a weekly prayer meeting, but were greatly used of God to encourage other parents who, likewise, were going through times of similar distress. How very pleased our Heavenly Father was to see such faith and obedience. The very situation Satan had devised to limit their witness was used by the Lord to display His overcoming and life-releasing power. God really does work every thing together for good, and the power of it can be expressed immediately, regardless of outward circumstances. *Jesus Christ is Lord of all—now!*

Many of the references which Jesus made to natural things (little sparrows, lilies of the field, etc.) undoubtedly were first appreciated in a spiritual sense when he was a teenager. The hill country back of Nazareth must have been well-known to Him as He communed with His Heavenly Father in the setting of His creation. Jesus never forgot his teenage years, and, in His humanity, has a warm understanding of the peculiar problems of young people. Most faithfully He had obeyed His earthly parents, and thereby learned the discipline which was necessary for His life to find its full and complete purpose.

Respect and obedience are qualities which are as essential for the welfare of society as a whole as at the level of the home. A spirit of rebellion and disrespect in the home which is not corrected in love and wisdom will ultimately produce a person who is sick on the inside. It is a sickness which will infect the world in which the individual lives, an observation which is too obvious perhaps for comfort.

Parental respect is related to the first commandment with promise—"that it may be well with thee, and thou mayest live long on the earth." The converse is a serious alternative which promises nothing less than death itself—spirit, soul, and body! Sadly, we see in our society today the consequences of God's broken commandment!

The Holy Spirit has come to minister life, not death, and, consequently, works into our lives the power and desire to honor and obey. There is no way this principle can be violated without forfeiting God's blessing and inviting the inevitable consequences. This is true at every level of family life, both heavenly and earthly. It is necessary to instill this truth into the lives of our children. Even Jesus had to learn the meaning of obedience, or He would have held back from the suffering of the cross. I believe these were lessons He learned initially as a boy in the various demands of family life.

There are Spirit-filled families who so emphasize the permissive side of God's love, they fail to realize there is also a decisive and corrective side as well. *God disciplines those whom He loves!* It is through obedience and discipline that the life principle of the cross is established in young hearts and lives. Sometimes parents can be almost intimidated by the Spirit of this age, which so emphasizes the generation gap that it is assumed any opposition to the desires of our young people will endanger our communication with them. Consequently, parental direction and control is no longer exercised, even though we may discern certain areas of activity as questionable; this tends toward a spiritual deterioration in the home.

Even as this was being written, a phone call arrived from a distressed mother whose son and daughter-in-law are caught up in one of the oriental cults. At one time both children had been Spirit-filled members of the church. They never learned, however, the discipline of the cross in their lives in their Christian walk. Even when they were children, there was such a permissive atmosphere in the home that their wills were seldom crossed. A part of this involved the kind of music they were allowed to bring into the home against the better judgment and spiritual discernment of their parents.

As has been considered in another chapter, we cannot avoid the cross without opening our lives to the delusion of the Enemy. Even the temptations of Jesus were designed to present the enticing possibility of an earthly kingdom apart from the price of the crucifixion. He refused to disobey His Heavenly Father, however, and firmly confessed His commitment to God's holy purpose for His life. "Thy will, not mine," is still the only way into resurrection life and truth. *Obedience is a sure defense against the deceptive power of the Devil.* God requires parents to stand firm concerning the principles of truth which He has designed for the spiritual welfare of the home!

I have endeavored to explain to my own children that I may not always be right in some judgments or decisions, for no one is infallible; yet, I expect them to obey. As parents we should endeavor to be careful in our demands and quick to admit an error in judgment when we discover it. This might even involve a reversal in decision! Surely this is a grace which the Holy Spirit can give to us in a practical way. Likewise, the Holy Spirit can give to the children the grace to obey even when they may disagree with their parents. In time, if parents and children are united in the Spirit, God can give a common ground of agreement which is pleasing to Him. Where better might we learn to appreciate the harmonizing power of the Spirit than in our homes?

To be filled with the Spirit is to fill our homes with the harmonizing Spirit of Jesus!

6

Truth and Error: Principles

The Scriptures clearly indicate that Satan is an exceptionally clever and powerful personality. I once referred to the Devil in a public meeting as being a fool. While there was a measure of truth in the statement within the context of the discussion, the Lord later impressed me never to underestimate his power for deception or to imply he was not a foe to be respected. In and of ourselves we will never be able to outwit or overpower our Adversary. His whole intention is to deceive and to destroy and thereby frustrate God's will and purpose for His family. In a most persistent and calculated way he subtly seeks to limit the life of Jesus from finding its full and intended expression in our daily lives.

OPPOSING THE POWER AND PSYCHOLOGY OF SATAN

Satan is a master psychologist—an expert student of human nature—and he clearly recognizes man's potential for evil when divorced from the love and power of God. The story of Job reveals to us that the Devil is not omniscient and his operation against man is in part a matter of maneuvering through an intelligent process of trial and error. He determines the weak areas in our character and corresponding deficiencies in our spiritual armor by approaching our lives in a variety of different ways. He will introduce thoughts into our minds and feelings into our hearts and then carefully watch our reactions. We live in a world which in its character is suffering from the consequences of sin and we see even in nature evidences of disorder, violence, and death. We are not immune from all of the accidents and reverses of everyday life. The Adversary observes our responses to such unavoidable distresses and soon has an accurate measure of our mental and emotional makeup. *Being familiar with our personality profile, he knows what avenues are open for his oppressive and deceptive powers!*

We must honestly recognize the possibility of our being deceived by the Devil if we do not rely on God's provisions for overcoming error. I recall reading the passage in Matthew 24:24, which speaks of false prophets endeavoring to "deceive the very elect," and feeling very sorry for all the elect around the world who were being deceived. Then it occurred to me that all the "deceived elect" probably were thinking the very same thing. The genius of deception is that the deceived don't realize it. *In fact, the most efficient deceiver is someone who doesn't know he is deceived himself!* He will be most convincing because no one will detect a note of insincerity in his message.

God has not left His people in a helpless, hopeless state of affairs, however, as if we are nothing more than a Yo-Yo on the end of the Devil's string. The Lord impressed me once that I did not have to jump through Satan's hoop every time he placed it in front of me. Actually, God has given us power by His Spirit, when we are rightly related to Him, to not only refuse to jump, but actually wrench the hoop from the hand of the Enemy and wring it around his neck!

The Lord has given to His people power over all the power of the Enemy (Luke 10:19). He also has provided us with both the gifts and principles of discernment that we might detect the Deceiver in his wily ways. Here we see God's Spirit and His truth working together on our behalf to spare us from the Devil's subtle snares. We will also come to appreciate the protecting power of the cross of Christ in both opposing and overcoming the Tempter. There is an interesting story in the Gospels which beautifully illustrates the principles discussed thus far. Let us see God's truth as it is translated into life!

DISCERNMENT THROUGH DISCIPLINE

Peter is an excellent example of a devoted disciple with a heavenly revelation from the Father above. His confession of faith concerning

Jesus as the Christ evoked a prompt and warm response on the part of our Lord. Peter the "rock," however, became a "stumbling stone" a few verses further on in our familiar story (Matt. 16:13-24). Here we see the same devoted disciple, completely unaware he had become an instrument of the Enemy, trying to convince Jesus to bypass the seeming tragedy of the cross. *His natural mind and human feelings had become the ground from which Satan endeavored to tempt Jesus to avoid the cross and thereby forfeit the triumph of the resurrection!*

Jesus immediately discerned the source of Peter's dissuasion and moved decisively and emphatically against the Devil with a sharp word of rebuke. His personal response to Peter is interesting in that it involves principles which relate to all of our lives when similar situations arise. Peter's deception became an occasion for instruction concerning the truth. Very carefully Jesus explained to him the necessity of the *cross principle* in the experience of every true disciple if the reality of His "life more abundant" was to be forthcoming in his daily walk with God.

It was my privilege to lead a young man and his fiancée into the baptism of the Holy Spirit one evening in the home of some former students. Both had been involved in the drug scene and he had recently been released from prison. With their subsequent marriage and his enrollment in the college where I was teaching, a whole new life opened up simultaneously on three fronts—church, school, and home! It was not without the expected adjustments and God used the problems to present the cross as the only gateway to true resurrection power. *The crown of life can never be achieved apart from the cross of death!* This has very personal and practical meaning which is both basic and essential to the Spirit-controlled life in Christ.

My young friend was an ardent and effective witness for Jesus Christ. His great delight was to share his faith on the beaches of Southern California. He would place his Bible on a mound of sand and soon have an interested and sympathetic audience as he testified about how Christ had changed his life. Many accepted the Lord as their Savior through his personal and persuasive witness. On the homefront and at school the situation was not quite so victorious. Personal adjustments with his new wife were lacking in the fruit of the Spirit. His academic responsibilities were suffering because of the time he was spending at the beach. Lessons were not learned, classes were cut or attended late, and a sense of responsibility was generally lacking.

One day he came by my office to discuss the frustration and confusion of feelings which by this time were becoming somewhat overwhelming. The Lord led us to consider the importance of Christian character and the way it is developed. God has a place of responsibility and a function in life for each one of us in the Christian community. This must be recognized and accepted if we are to be Christ's disciples and mastered by His Spirit. *To be a "disciple" literally means to become a "disciplined one."*

When we willingly submit to the discipline and direction of the Holy Spirit, He gives us the power and desire to "die out" to any diverting or distracting impulses in our lives. Like our Lord, we set our face like a flint toward our "Jerusalem," and without flinching or swerving, joyfully and gladly walk with Him all the way. Not everyone has the privilege of taking up his cross and following Jesus into such resurrection life and power!

In our discussion, God made it very clear that the "cross-and-crown" life was more than lofty idealism or sentimental thinking. *The Holy Spirit is a very practical Person whose power can bring eternal purpose to every part of our daily lives!* I shared with him an interesting lesson we had learned at the home of some Spirit-filled friends. After morning devotions with his family, one of the children announced he was going out to dig weeds from the yard. Another one of the boys added with a laugh that at least they would be working on holy ground. (The entire place had been dedicated to God.) In an unexpected way the Holy Spirit moved upon one of the young ladies present and she softly responded in a manifestation of tongues. There followed an interpretation informing us that God is indeed as close to us as is the very ground upon which we walk. There is not one step in our daily lives which does not touch the Lord if we love Him and confess we have been called according to His purpose. Furthermore, the Spirit indicated to us that He takes the earthly circumstances surrounding our lives to bring forth His heavenly purpose through our lives. We were reminded that when God created Adam, it was the dust of this earth which He fashioned and into which He breathed the breath of life.

In other words, God was trying to shape my student friend into the image of Jesus through the very circumstances and responsibilities he was trying to avoid. I explained to him that while student chapel would be a source of inspiration and direction, his home and classroom would be the setting for most of his character building. He then expressed a desire to really become a "disciplined one" and "die out" to his tendency to live life without restraint or responsibility. How fortunate this young man was to learn early in his Christian walk that the cross is the gateway to true personal fulfillment!

SELF-REALIZATION THROUGH SURRENDER

We can really find ourselves only as we first lose ourselves in Jesus!
This has some very practical applications in our daily personal affairs.
We must be willing to die out to any ambition, desire, or confidence
which does not have its origin in God. This includes all thoughts,
passions, and imaginations which are not sanctioned by the Holy Spirit.
As will be explained later, it often takes the releasing power of the Holy
Spirit to *also* yield to the cross our fears, doubts, torments, and
depressions! As we do however, we find ourselves gloriously free in the
resurrection life of Jesus!

As simple and obvious as this may seem, many Christians have been
deceived by the Enemy into embracing one of two extremes
concerning their lives, both of which bypass God's chosen way.
Currently there is a rash of books, lectures, and group sessions centered
around the theme of self-realization. The emphasis is on knowing,
accepting, and expressing oneself. Personal inhibitions are recognized
and overcome by honest appraisal coupled with positive thinking,
followed by decisive remedial action. The process may even involve
prayer and a mixed emphasis on faith in God and self. The cross-life as
defined by Jesus is carefully avoided, however.

Now such a program will produce results, but it must be remembered that water rises no higher than its own level. *The self-realization
of self has built-in limitations!* Some years ago my wife and I were
staying at the home of a Spirit-filled surgeon. In the evening he came
home aglow with the joy of a wonderful testimony. A man had come to
him for spiritual counsel and confessed his desire to find God for his
life. The gentleman had obtained a number of books related to religious
science and metaphysics and with enthusiasm he explained what a
change for the better the principles involved had brought to his home
and daily life.

At first my surgeon-friend said his heart sank when he learned what
a deceptive path the man had taken. But, as he drew upon the Spirit of
wisdom and truth, he heard himself say, "That's just fine, and such
principles will really work well as far as the things of time are
concerned, but apart from Christ they won't produce a thing that will
count for eternity. What you really want is eternal life which can be
found only in the redemptive work of Jesus on the cross!" The man's
heart had already been prepared by the Holy Spirit and he immediately
responded by accepting Christ into his life as Lord and Savior. That
night he came to the home to be filled with the Holy Spirit and it was

our joy to pray with him.

The Lord impressed me later concerning the power which is resident in man's mind and soul. Men have built empires and unlocked the mysteries of nature by developing its potential. But at his best man can never break through the barriers of sin that hold him back from that which is heavenly, eternal, and divinely spiritual. *Apart from the cross of Christ and the power of God's Spirit, man is an earthbound, time-bound, mind-bound and sin-bound creature!* Man has an eternal and spiritual destiny which can never be realized by either his intellect or innate goodness alone. He will never find himself apart from Jesus. Only as he becomes personally acquainted with the Savior can he truly become acquainted with himself. In Christ we see both what we are not, and what we can become. Here is life as it is meant to be lived . . . forever!

The other extreme may also be expressed within a religious guise. It is the deception that the truly noble life is characterized by a self-mortification which almost borders on psychological suicide. Some individuals are plagued with a sense of worthlessness from which they dare not extract themselves lest they commit the mortal sin of self-exaltation. They seemingly are on the horns of a dilemma. Either direction theoretically results in the elimination of their selfhood. Such a position fails to see there is a difference between "self-denial" and the eradication of personality.

Jesus didn't come to eliminate us as unique identities (as is the objective of many Oriental cults) but rather to set us free to become ourselves in Him! This involves submitting and surrendering our selves to the sovereignty of the Holy Spirit that God's heavenly and eternal purpose *for* us can be fulfilled *through* us—here on earth in time. Again we see the practical and personal side of the Holy Spirit's ministry. As we die out to being centered in self, we find the fountainhead of our being in Christ. He is the integrating theme which relates all the various aspects of our lives most uniquely into God's eternal plan and pleasure! To be self-centered (either in the extreme of realization or mortification) rather than self-surrendered, is to be excluded from the joy of taking up our cross daily and following Jesus into His life more abundant.

It takes the releasing and sanctifying power of the Holy Spirit to transfer the truth of the cross-life into personal experience! Apart from Him it is impossible to work up even a decent dedication. We are always wondering if our consecration and surrender to God is acceptable. The "law of the Spirit of life in Christ Jesus" lifts us from the heaviness and weakness of such introspection and brings us to the powerful simplicity of the "filled-to-overflowing" life which Christ promised to those who would believe (John 7:37-39; Rom. 8:1-16; Gal. 5:16-25). Again as we shall see, this is most personal and most practical.

SOME PERSONAL TESTIMONIES

Recently my wife and I had the privilege of sharing and praying together with two Roman Catholic sisters during a weekend retreat in the mountains. We were all seated in the restful atmosphere of the surrounding pine trees, which have always been a symbol and source of peace and freedom for me. It was a warm, sunny day softened by the spring breezes which so delightfully sing their way through the trees of the high country.

The lives of these two lovely sisters, however, were far from that which speaks of inner peace and joy. Both were devoted to Jesus and had sought for years to please Him not only by denying themselves many of the usual comforts and freedoms of life, but by deliberately depreciating and suppressing their God-given personalities. Both were rather joyful and very loving in a natural, outgoing way which demanded expression beyond the limitations they had placed upon their lives by their religious calling. Years of frustration and inner conflict had produced both emotional and physical illness. One had required both psychiatric and medical attention. Both had sought the baptism of Jesus in the Holy Spirit, but lingering questions plus a heavy hold from fears and misconceptions of the past hindered the full release of the Spirit through their lives.

We shared with them the understanding that Spirit-baptism involves an immersion that is to touch every area of life experience with the releasing power of the living Christ. This includes the past as well as the present. I related an experience God had given to a lady we had prayed with some years earlier. She had requested a ministry of deliverance from fear. Her face was clouded and joyless and she obviously needed to be released both in spirit and in soul (mentally and emotionally). Rather than praying immediately, I felt prompted to share with her the faithful and powerful ministry of the Holy Spirit which can lift us beyond our own limitations.

God knows us better than we know ourselves and where we might fail in trying to diagnose the source of our problems, He will not. Furthermore, He is not interested in merely treating symptoms, but in reaching into the very root of our need, whether it be in our conscious or subconscious life; whether it be in the past, present, or an imaginary projection for the future. *The baptism of Jesus is to touch every part of our life experience!* We then prayed together that the searching and releasing Spirit of God would meticulously move through her life from past to present. Every part of the past was to be reached—people, places, decisions, mistakes, failures, disappointments, hurts, evil influences . . . everything! Nothing would be left untouched!

If we saw that at any point an evil force or power had gained access to her life, we immediately confessed not only the dispelling power of God but the presiding presence of the living Christ. We pictured the Lord opening the drapes and throwing open the windows of her soul that He who is the light of the whole world would become the light of her life. No dark corners or lingering shadows were to remain. The clear, bright, white light of the Lord was to search out every recess and compartment of her being until she became perfectly and gloriously transparent before Him. The fresh, pure breath of God was to revive and restore her staleness of soul and mustiness of mind. The rushing stream of truth was seen as washing through her conscious and subconscious, bringing a healing to her memory. No longer would the thoughts of the past bring pain, torment or condemnation. Jesus was setting her free!

Where past pride, hatred, jealousy, or resentment had found a foothold, we proclaimed the overcoming power of humility, love, compassion, and forgiveness. Personalities involved in the above feelings were released to the grace of God that they too might have their lives touched by His. The liberating work of the Holy Spirit once again was setting a child of God free!

So intense was God's power that the woman actually fell to the floor from her chair and joyfully began praising God in other tongues. I assured her startled husband that everything was all right and that God had indeed answered our prayers. She praised God fluently in the Spirit some time before resuming her prayer in English. Whereupon she exclaimed over and over again, "Oh, my Redeemer, my King, my Lord!" She finally climaxed her worship with these beautiful words, "Welcome home, Oh, welcome home!" The last I saw of her, her husband was helping her out the door as she was half lost in the Spirit. I can still see her hand raised in worship and hear her joyfully confessing that Jesus was indeed her "Lord of Lords and King of Kings"!

The two sisters with whom we were sharing this story requested that they too might experience this inner healing and release for their lives. How very great was their need and desire to really find their freedom in Christ. God had already lifted their faith to a place of holy expectation, so we simply joined our hands and hearts in prayer for each of them. Once again the healing hands of Jesus touched the lives of two of His beloved sisters, as a pine tree and a stone bench became our altar of worship. There was laughter and there were tears, all from hearts overflowing with the joy of the Lord. My wife and I were hugged and blessed profusely and I am sure the angels joined their voices with ours as we sang the song of a soul set free! Subsequent sharing with the two sisters proved the depth and validity of the Spirit's work; the joy and inner release has been lasting.

Perhaps you as the reader have felt your heart burn within you as you have read these words. That is the releasing work of the Holy Spirit bearing witness to the truth. You too can be set free this way this very moment. God is no respecter of persons or places. Reread the above paragraphs making each statement a personal prayer and confession. As you do, the mighty rushing river of God's Spirit will set you free . . . now! I can feel the power and authority of His presence as I write, and I know that faith brings the same witness to your own heart and soul. Praise Him profusely for your newfound freedom in Christ. What a joyful confession can be ours now: "If the Son therefore shall make you free, ye shall be free indeed!"

PRINCIPLES OF DISCERNMENT

In traveling about the country and also overseas I became aware that the Enemy has particular patterns of activity designed to deceive God's people and thereby bring limitation, confusion, and division. The Apostle Paul exhorts us not to be ignorant of his devices, so let us consider some of the subtle snares which he cunningly employs. We will also see God's answer to deception which involves both discernment and deliverance. Discernment is based on both spiritual gifts and principles of truth.

Spiritual discernment is a ministry of the Holy Spirit in line with the principles of God's Word whereby we can distinguish between truth and error, light and darkness, life and death, peace and turmoil in the spiritual realm. It is necessary to recognize what is from the heart and mind (affections and understanding) of God, in contrast to that which is derived from the will and pleasure of man and/or Satan. Man can be most persuasive in a strong, soulish way, and the Devil can appear as an "angel of light" to the unsuspecting saint. Some situations may convey strong influences from all three sources and present a most confusing picture!

The motivating power behind all of our actions stems from these three centers: God, man, or Satan. The earlier reference to Peter is an excellent example of all three. At one moment he is confessing the Sonship of Christ, and the next he is speaking as "from the mind of man," and becomes the channel through which Satan himself once again tempts Jesus to bypass the cross.

SPIRITUALITY VERSUS SOULISHNESS

A brief discussion concerning the makeup of man would be meaningful at this point. The Bible sometimes uses the words "soul" and "spirit" synonymously and at other times seems to differentiate between the two. In the distinctive sense, the spirit (pneuma) of man, apart from the ministry of the Holy Spirit, is represented as being lifeless to the heavenly, eternal, and divinely spiritual realm. Man's spirit when quickened by God's Spirit, however, can receive divine revelation and/or illumination; it can respond in prayer, praise, confession, and intercession; it can engage in spiritual witness and warfare and share in the communion of saints; it also becomes the faculty for spiritual discernment.

The soul (psyche) of man may be defined as the seat of personality as it relates to the temporal, earthly, and natural conditions of life. It is the fountainhead of reason, volition, affection, memory, imagination, conscience, and perception of sensory stimuli. Apart from the control of the Holy Spirit, interacting with and through man's spirit, the soulish functions of man cannot apprehend, express, or relate to heavenly purpose. The soul is geared to the spirit of this world and becomes the ground upon which the Enemy of our souls opposes the things of God. Soulish functions, separated from the life and power of God's Holy Spirit, produce character and conduct described in the Scriptures under such terms as: fleshly, carnal, unregenerate, and natural. (Rom. 8; I Cor. 2; Gal. 5 *Amplified Bible*).

Man also has a body (soma) by which he relates to and interacts with the natural world around him. He senses out the character of his living and nonliving environment and responds either reflexively or reflectively in what is usually a life-promoting fashion. All three aspects of man's being are interrelated and integrated by design into a meaningful whole.

Man lives in a body, but he is more than a body. He has a soul, but he is more than a soul. He is also a spiritual being! When our spirit is alive and submissive to God's Spirit, the soul is inspired to uniquely express the life of Jesus through our physical body to the world without. *In this way, through man, the earthly things of time and nature are related to God's heavenly, spiritual, and eternal purposes!*

No wonder Satan would deceive us into living a limited, two-dimensional, soulish-sensual life apart from God's Spirit. He seeks to disconnect us from our divine destiny and thereby frustrate the will of our heavenly Father. We are not helpless victims of the Devil's deceptive powers, however—Jesus has seen to that! He has sent to us His Holy Spirit and among His many gifts are those of discernment and deliverance.

We can by God's Spirit discern when the Deceiver is trying to tempt us to "think it through alone" rather than "reasoning together" with God. We will recognize His persistent pressure to focus our faith in our *feelings* rather than the word and life of our Lord. No longer will we view with fear the fantasies Satan paints upon the canvas of our *imaginations.* The paralyzing pain of past *memories* has been healed by the power of God's Holy Spirit. We can actively oppose the Accuser's attempt to strike our *conscience* with the spirit of condemnation. We can joyfully confess that God will work together for good everything that we might *perceive* with alarm or anxiety concerning our natural earthly circumstances. Truly the "law of the spirit of life in Christ Jesus has set us free . . .!"

With these principles in mind we will see the spirit of truth sharply separating that which is soulish and that which is spiritual in the various problem situations which we shall discuss in the next chapter. We can also further appreciate the meaning of the cross in our daily walk with Christ. As we obediently submit in faith to the perfecting power of the Holy Spirit in our lives, we will simultaneously discover we are "dying out" to soulish powers and pleasures. As we learn to "live in the Spirit," we will become more and more sensitive to that which does or does not produce the life, light, peace, and joy of Jesus! This is the basis of true discernment in Christ.

THE PURPOSE OF DISCERNMENT

We should consider first of all the purpose for which discernment is given. With it comes a great responsibility for us to play a redemptive role in the lives of those about us. The Adversary will oppose our participation in such redemptive effrots by enticing us into the dead-end roads of pride, guilt, or indifference.

The purpose for which the Spirit gives discernment will be frustrated if we allow ourselves to be elevated to a place of pride because we have detected something amiss in a given situation. This can be a particular danger when we share our feeling with others for the purpose of confirmation. There can be a subtle sense of elation that will lay hold of our lives if we are not careful when we discover that someone or a group of individuals have deviated from or fallen short of God's intended purpose in some way. All of us have been tempted along these lines at one time or another and have discovered that genuine discernment can deteriorate into a spirit of criticism coupled with self-exaltation. The grieving Spirit of God can never lay a ministry of intercessory prayer upon a proud person—the redemptive purpose for our discernment will be completely frustrated.

What a paradox is presented when we can seemingly discern everything but pride in our own lives! I know of a man of God who had a remarkable ministry of deliverance which was directed to individuals who had come under demonic influence of one type or another. A false sense of self-confidence developed which required a ministry of deliverance on his own behalf. How readily we realize that there can be no substitute for the ministry of the cross in our daily lives. *Within its shadow is great safety!*

Pride can obviously destroy God's purpose for discernment but so can a contrasting sense or feeling of guilt. The Devil may try to raise doubts and questions concerning our discernment in an endeavor to deceive us. We may be aware in our spirit something is amiss before we recognize what it is at the level of our understanding. In spite of what we sense *within* there may be apparent blessing and success *without.* Much truth and love may even be evident, but yet there is that little red flag of the Spirit which persistently flutters in the periphery of our vision. Others may seem to be oblivious to any signal of danger and joyfully participate in the rising waves of enthusiasm.

At this point we may be tempted to doubt our sensitivity to the Spirit and feel we have fallen heir to an envious, critical, judgmental attitude toward our brothers and sisters. With this comes a paralyzing sense of guilt which renders us useless as far as God's redemptive purpose is concerned. If we try to disclaim our discernment and go along with the situation in a way which implies our endorsement, we find ourselves in a place of great inner conflict and agony of soul. What is God's answer?

First of all it is always safe to begin at the cross and honestly ask the

Lord to reveal to us any soulish shadows of pride, envy, or ctiticism which may obscure our spiritual vision and confuse our judgment. If after our own lives are cleared, our uneasiness of spirit persists, we should hold fast in faith to our discernment and respond in intercessory prayer. This may be as far as our responsibility goes. On the other hand, God may focus our understanding and require we move decisively in a ministry of restoration. This will involve the graces of love, patience, and humility, coupled with such gifts as knowledge, wisdom, and faith. These are expressions of the Spirit which will enable us to move with God in a right way, and at the right time with the right people for His redemptive purpose!

GOD'S SPIRIT: A PURIFYING FLAME

It is possible as mentioned above to experience situations in which there seems to be a mixture of spiritual blessing and soulish success. One grieves at the violation of spiritual and occasionally ethical principles, yet is confused by the apparent blessing of God in both material and spiritual ways in spite of it all. Great anguish of heart will accompany any endeavor to reconcile in our minds that which cannot be spiritually reconciled!

God brought a measure of understanding to me through His Word concerning such conflicts and later confirmed it one evening by a prophetic word after I had retired. The fourteenth chapter of I Chronicles relates the story of David's desire to return the Ark of God to its rightful place of recognition in the city of Jerusalem. God had ordained the way in which the ark was to be moved from one place to another—it was to be carried by means of poles upon the shoulders of the Levites! The Levitical priesthood represents the spiritual power and authority which is ever the source of divine life for God's people!

David substituted for the priesthood a Philistine mode of transportation—a new ox-driven cart! In a soulish sense it was a reasonable, rapid method of moving the ark along. The occasion began in a highly successful way. David, God's anointed king, was leading the procession. His motives and purpose were seemingly sincere and straightforward. All the notables and leaders in the entire congregation of Israel were present. There was singing, dancing, and much music. One wonders, however, if some sensitive man of God might not have discerned that all was not as well as the apparent blessing would suggest. Was he perhaps intimidated by the majority who failed to recognize that a right thing was being accomplished in a wrong way? Was he silent when he should have spoken? Or was his voice ignored as one who couldn't relate to the corporate effort?

The cart moved swiftly toward Jerusalem and our man of God may have wondered if perhaps his judgment had been wrong. Maybe God isn't as particular concerning His principles as had been thought. Then it happened! In one last extreme attempt to stop the procession, God seemingly was prepared to knock the ark to the ground. The oxen stumbled and the ark slid toward the side. A man lifted a fleshy hand to steady the ark and was immediately struck dead by God! (I am sure Uzzah was taken to Paradise, but what a tragic way to go).

It all happened by the threshing floor of Chidon. It was a bitter and painful lesson for David, but a necessary one. If the soulish seeds of doing God's will in man's way had not been uprooted at the very outset, David's temple for a Holy God never would have been built! The spiritual source which provided the wisdom and authority for its erection would long since have departed. The same is true today. There is a temple of living stones which is rising heavenward, and is to be destined to be an eternal habitation for the Spirit of the Living God (Eph. 2:22). We are those living stones!

Our journey to Jerusalem also passes by the threshing floor. John the Baptist prophetically pictured it in this way: "He [Jesus] will baptize you with fire—and with the Holy Spirit. He will separate chaff from grain, and burn up the chaff with eternal fire and store away the grain" (Luke 3:16-17 *Living Gospels*). To put it another way, *every stone in God's Holy Temple is going to be fire-polished!*

One night the Lord impressed me in the Spirit that He was going to be moving in an extensive and intensive way in these last days. It is a work which will be done both in and through His people—the living Church! I questioned if this meant the character-building work of the cross was going to be bypassed since this involves time and testing. *He assured me no one could avoid the cross and still fulfill his destiny anymore than Jesus could have bypassed the cross and fulfilled His!* I was impressed, however, that God looks at the inclination of our hearts rather than outward appearances, and where He finds wholehearted men who have set their life toward His will, there He intends to do an accelerated work.

Yes, the Holy Spirit will be moving as a purifying flame reducing to ashes everything in our lives which is soulish in origin so only that which finds its fountainhead in heaven will remain. This will be true both in a corporate and in an individual sense. This He will accomplish in His way and in His time, but it is as inevitable as the light that accompanies the rising sun. Truly, this is the dawning of a new day—the day of the Lord!

DANGER: POLLUTED WATERS

Only the clean, clear streams of the Spirit are everlasting in quality. There is a spiritual ecology which is as violently opposed to pollution as are the principles of a sound earthly ecology. It is not without purpose that air and water are types of the Holy Spirit. No wonder the prophet Micah warned God's people not to be at ease in the midst of contaminating influences. "Arise and go away: for this is no place for your rest, because the pollution will bring destruction, and the destruction will be grievous" (Mic. 2:10 Lamsa).

The Apostle James raises a question concerning fountains that send forth sweet and bitter water at the same time. Such "pollution" ought not so to be! (Jas. 3:10-11). Again we recognize the answer is in the cleansing work of the cross and the sanctifying power of the Spirit which never operate apart from each other. The story of the "bitter waters" of Marah (Exod. 15:23-26), which the Israelites experienced on their way to the Promised Land, seems to refer to those situations in life which force the "bitter roots" hidden within to spring forth in a most evident and obvious way. It took a "tree" provided by God to sweeten the waters at Marah. It likewise takes the "cross" to sweeten and sanctify the fruitful overflow of our daily lives!

The writer of Hebrews correlates these thoughts in these words, "Continue to live in peace with everyone and pursue that purity and holiness of life without which no one will ever see the Lord. Look after each other so that not one of you will fail to find God's best blessings. Watch out that no poisonous root of bitterness springs up among you and thereby contaminates the whole community" (Heb. 12:14-15 various translations). How thankful we can be for the patient, persistent, purifying power of God's Holy Spirit!

To be filled with the Spirit is to know the discerning and delivering power that Christ and His cross can bring to our daily lives!

7

Truth and Error: Problems

With the principles discussed in our last chapter now set in our hearts, let us consider some of the problem areas where Satan's deceptive power is most prevalent.

SOULISH MYSTICISM

One subtle form of soulish behavior is a pseudo-spiritual emphasis that can lead to an unwholesome mysticism. There usually is a great emphasis upon new revelations and spiritual mysteries often accompanied by visions, dreams, and "prophetic" discourses.

Truly, there is hidden truth in God's Word which the Holy Spirit desires to reveal to the diligent seeker. The last days surely will be accompanied by dreams, visions, and prophecy as Peter's Pentecostal message clearly promises. All such manifestations, however, must be tested by God's Word and discerning Spirit. A further and very practical proof of validity is the fruit produced. If a proud, exclusive feeling develops based on secret and superior revelations which only those who have "pressed on" in the Spirit can appreciate, there is danger ahead! Such groups and individuals are inclined to isolate themselves from others, and soon develop a very unteachable spirit.

There will also be a tendency to drift away from the responsibility of sharing Jesus with others as Savior and Baptizer. Such ministry is subconsciously considered elementary and not as satisfying as searching out new mysteries. Home meetings which currently may be very fruitful in reaching the basic spiritual needs of God's children can deteriorate into sterile, inbred fellowships primarily centered around sharing new revelations.

God always wishes to translate truth into life, and there is great safety in allowing the cross to test out our spiritual direction by the fruit it produces in our interpersonal relationships at home, school, work, and the Christian community at large. *We are not really heavenly minded at all if we are so disconnected from this world that we are of no earthly use to God.*

Anything which competes with our daily communion with Jesus and the joy of sharing His life with others can lead to outright error. To become so preoccupied with the supernatural that such manifestations take on a soulish delight can set us up for the lying signs and wonders of the Devil (II Thess. 2:9). All supernatural manifestations are not of God. The Deceiver has counterfeits for all of the spiritual gifts. (Suggested reading: Ralph Gasson, *The Challenging Counterfeit.* Logos International, 185 North Avenue, Plainfield, New Jersey, 07060.)

So-called spiritual leaders have been seduced into spiritism by approaching the occult from an intellectual (but soulish) point of view. To investigate out of curiosity even the borderline areas of parapsychology apart from the spiritual defenses is to invite deception and delusion into one's life. It has happened, but needlessly so!

The same could be said for those who out of curiosity submit themselves to the mystery cults of the East. Inherent in these systems is a deceptive power which in the guise of love and truth will darken the souls of those involved. For some the teachings may appear to be nothing more than interesting oriental philosophy, but for others they become an open door to demonic forces which require an authoritative ministry of deliverance. No wonder the Apostle Paul warned the Corinthian believers lest by any means they be deceived by the subtlety of the serpent and become corrupted *in their minds* away from the simplicity that is in Christ Jesus (II Cor. 11:3).

PREOCCUPATION WITH SIGNS

There is another natural tendency which can develop as we become warmly aware of God's hand at work in our daily lives; that is, to see or seek to see supernatural signs at every point along our way. *Coincidence*

may or may not be Providence and we need to discern the difference!
Biblical numerology is both interesting and profitable, but to read
spiritual significance into *every* number which is seen throughout our
daily experiences borders on superstition.

The Lord impressed a group of us with His feeling on this matter one
evening. We had arrived at a home prayer-and-share meeting after
attending a local PTA program. The meeting was under way and, as we
discovered later, my wife and I sensed something was not completely in
the flow of God's Spirit. Someone had raised a question concerning
God's will in a forthcoming decision and the suggestion had been made
that she seek a specific sign of His leading. An element of superstition
was subtly mixed into the discussion, and a state of spiritual confusion
soon developed.

Suddenly, a lady who had just recently been filled with the Holy
Spirit spoke out in a manifestation of tongues. It was like soothing oil
upon troubled waters. The interpretation was in the form of an
exhortation. The Lord impressed us to be careful in our pursuit of signs
lest we become misguided by the false signs of the Enemy. We were
cautioned about shifting our faith from God's greatest Sign (Jesus) to
that of earthly signs. Our confidence was to rest primarily upon our
Good Shepherd rather than on some method of determining God's will.
We were assured that the Lord knew just when and where to encourage
us with natural signs and would enable us to discern their divine
placement. We all recognized the Lord's love and wisdom and accepted
His constructive counsel.

The method of setting out "fleeces" to confirm God's will, as
Gideon did, seems more of an expression of doubt than faith. (Judg.
6:36-40). God had already given His word, but Gideon still wanted two
signs he could see before he would believe. Perhaps God in His grace
still condescends to our Gideon-like weaknesses at such times of need,
but desires a greater expression of faith as we mature. The important
principle in guidance is that our faith be fixed primarily in the
faithfulness of our Great Shepherd who assures us His sheep will hear
His voice. Signs, fleeces, and all other indications then will find their
proper place in our lives.

This is not to rule out the possibility that the Spirit may prompt us
on occasion to consider a certain possible "turn of events" as a sign
from the Lord that our expectation is in faith. *Even here our "sign"
will be subjected to the principles of truth revealed in God's Word and
the inner witness of His discerning Spirit.*

There are times when there will be no signs forthcoming at all until we move out in faith and obedience in the direction our heart's desire indicates. The Scripture declares (Ps. 37:4) that if our delight is in being led of God's Spirit, He will give us the desires of our heart. (This can well mean He is substituting our desires for His.) Often God waits for us to explore in faith the "little leading" that we have before revealing more of His will. *What is of God, He will bless by bringing forth the life of Jesus!*

My wife and I, after months of praying for God's will concerning a change, were becoming weary with waiting. The only answer I received was that in the process we were becoming better acquainted with The One upon whom we waited! Finally, the opportunity came most unexpectedly. It involved a major move to the West Coast and we wanted to be sure it was really of the Lord. All of the necessary practical considerations for moving the family had rather miraculously been provided for. Still we wanted that final witness from God's Word.

The "desire of our heart" was to share the reality of the Spirit-filled life with those who had no "Pentecostal" background. Finally, I discovered this promise in Paul's writings: "For it is God Himself who creates within you both the desire and the power to execute His gracious will" (Phil. 2:13 paraphrase). We made our move on the basis of this, believing if this was not His will and desire, He would let us know. This was the turning point in our lives that led to the experiences that prompted the writing of this book. We could never have anticipated how that desire was going to unfold beyond anything we had ever seen in the past. Praise God, He is a Good Shepherd!

"And though the Lord give you the bread of adversity and the water of affliction, yet your teacher will not hide Himself anymore, but your eyes will constantly behold your Teacher. And your ears shall hear a word behind you, saying, This is the way, walk ye in it, when you turn to the right hand and when you turn to the left" (Isa. 30:20-21 *Amplified Bible*).

THE LORD IS MY SHEPHERD

One day the Lord impressed me with this question: "Why are you following so many different shepherds?" Upon reflection I realized that whenever I faced a decision or was in a place of spiritual evaluation, I subconsciously was looking more to people than to God. Now there is safety in a multitude of counselors (Prov. 11:14), and the wisdom of mature saints is to be sought and respected; but never should such a privilege become a substitute for counsel with the Good Shepherd Himself. *In the final analysis God will hold us directly and personally responsible for our walk with Him!*

There is a tendency for us all and especially for the newly Spirit-baptized believer to be greatly impressed by individuals with highly gifted ministries. Such men and women of God are to be highly respected for they have been placed in the body of Christ for its profit. Often such Godly saints play a significant role in our relationship with God, and we turn to them readily in our early stages of growth. *There will come a time, however, when the Lord will wean us away from our initial dependency upon people to a more mature relationship of faith in Him.* The weaning process can be painful until we discern what God is doing.

Many times God has placed His "angels of mercy and wisdom" in my path just when I needed them most. I am grateful to the Lord for the gracious gifts of His Spirit which I have received from saintly brothers and sisters. Truly "a word fitly spoken is like apples of gold in pictures of silver" (Prov. 25:11). On other occasions, however, I have sought in a soulish way for God's word of wisdom from some gifted individual I presumed was most qualified to minister to my need—only to be greatly disappointed!

Several times I have been treated almost rudely (not intentionally) by my intended benefactors until I finally realized what God was doing. I remember one godly saint walking off to embrace an old friend just as I was in the middle of an important question which I felt only he could answer. I was left standing alone—with the Lord! In my mind's eye I could see Him looking at me rather knowingly. I responded with a sheepish smile, but didn't say anything. Nothing needed to be said; the lesson was clear!

There will be times when others may become dependent upon us in what may become an unwholesome relationship, spiritually speaking. *True spiritual leadership will lead men to a healthy relationship with Christ which they can share with others rather than a developing dependency upon the leader.*

I recall a foreign student whom I had helped in many ways through prayer and counsel at critical times. It was a pleasure to see him mature into a godly minded young man. After we had decided to make a change of teaching positions, he came by my office to inquire if we were really leaving. He then told me in a touching way that I had been a "spiritual father" to him and how very sorry and discouraged he was to learn that I would no longer be there. I was greatly moved and must admit I shed some tears after he left. Then the Lord reminded me that this was a painful but necessary juncture in his walk with God. Our warm relationship would continue, but in a more wholesome way for the young man. God was making him to become a strong saint who would one day be lending a helping hand to others.

DOMINATING PERSONALITIES

"O Lord our God, other lords beside thee have had dominion over us, but thy name alone will we mention" (Isa. 26:13 Lamsa). The Lord has impressed me to be very careful never to depreciate the dignity of personality or to violate the freedom of choice concerning spiritual things which is the privilege of every individual. God honors the sovereignty of man in this sense and will assume control of our lives only by invitation. *The Lord is not a divine dictator who assumes command by force!*

There are spiritual dictators, however, who consciously or unconsciously exert a powerful controlling influence over the lives of others. Some are benevolent in behavior and basic intent and rarely express a strong, soulish spirit unless their position is challenged. Such individuals are often highly gifted in the Spirit and, without fully realizing it in some cases, utilize spiritual manifestations as a means of establishing their authority. *We all have a tendency to elevate charismatic personalities to a place of power and prestige which is good neither for them nor for us.* Many godly people have succumbed to the illusion that they were immune from error because men proclaimed them as infallible. Being deceived themselves, they have deceived others into following their every word without question.

God warned me that His blessing and gifts through our lives could never be a substitute for the work of the cross! This means descending from any man-made pedestals constructed by others. There is an authority and a position which the Lord gives His ministers which needs no embellishment by man. Only that which is grounded in God will survive the shaking which all of us are going to experience as the purifying power of the Holy Spirit loosens us from everything that is unacceptable and displeasing to Him (Heb. 12:27-29).

When I was first baptized into the Holy Spirit and recognized the reality of the spiritual gifts, I was not aware that such manifestations can sometimes have a soulish element which will not minister His life and sometimes not even align with the truth. If anyone indicated God had told them something or added a "thus saith the Lord" to a spoken utterance, I immediately accepted it as the gospel truth! The Scriptures declare we are not to despise or depreciate prophecy but to test and prove out all things and hold fast to that which is good (I Thess. 5:20-21).

This does not mean we are always probing everything with a suspicious spirit, but rather continually trusting the Spirit of discernment and truth to alert us to anything not from the Lord. *A prophetic utterance is not to be measured in terms of how loud, long, fluent, or flowery it is, but rather how much life, love, and truth it expresses!* I have heard prophecies that have brought much comfort and direction in the Lord and which were most alive with God's Spirit. Others, sadly, were so soulish in origin they ministered nothing but death and confusion.

God holds us responsible for the decisions of life. Never can we allow another, even through a prophetic word, to be the final authority concerning the direction for our lives. Any word which is truly from the Lord will have a confirming witness in our spirit from God's Spirit. *Furthermore, it is a witness which will last long enough to be confirmed in other ways!* Some in times past have allowed others to influence their decisions at critical times because they were afraid to question some so-called "spiritual" revelation or the person or group who received it! Consequences in some cases have been tragic.

Many times in teaching and sharing with others (and it applies throughout this book) the Lord has prompted me to instruct the people to accept only what they discern is a ministry from the Spirit. *We are not responsible before the Lord to walk in the light of another person's relationship with God!* We are held accountable only for the light which God gives us and to which His Spirit bears witness. We must learn to trust our Good Shepherd in a direct personal way, or sooner or later we will be led astray in some area by persuasive influences which are not of God. There are times when we need to be delivered from people as much as from the Devil!

My wife went to a meeting where a visiting couple was invited to share. They quickly controlled the time of worship and established a sense of authority and leadership by "prophetic" utterances which were rather harsh and judgmental. The wife of the couple then announced emphatically that God had given her a "ministry of reproof" and she discerned that the group was bound by a spirit of pride. She then declared that God would have them literally humble themselves by kneeling on the floor in repentance. A few of the ladies, who sweetly loved Jesus, were so intimidated by such a strong, soulish presentation, they submitted to the demand in fear and bewilderment. Others were confused, and some left. Here was a situation that required responsible and decisive action firmly based on sound principles of discernment. God in His grace used the incident as a means of instruction for all concerned.

IMPROPER PERSONAL RELATIONSHIPS

There is an important area of deception which must be considered in a rather direct and decisive manner. It involves friendships and other personal relationships which begin innocently enough but develop in an unwholesome way. The common occurrence and similarity of pattern of such problems indicates this is one of the Enemy's ways of insinuating Himself into the very midst of an otherwise beautiful family fellowship in the Lord. The "agape" love relationship between the members of a Christian community is the supreme seal of the Father's approval and blessing. It is not surprising, therefore, that Satan would subtly seek to pervert this relationship.

In his attempt to deprave the holy beauty of Christian friendship, the Deceiver seeks to beguile those involved by appearing as an angel of light. Initially, this is usually in the form of simple rationalization which, if entertained, will become sufficiently elaborate to excuse whatever behavior satisfies their thriving passions. Even relationships which are held short of overt sin can seriously weaken the spiritual life of those involved as well as the community as a whole. Even one-sided "imaginary" affairs indulged in by a single individual can influence others. The Scriptures indicate that where one member of the body of Christ suffers, all suffer with it. *No Christian lives a life unto himself without influencing others in one way or another.* This is a serious responsibility!

Let us consider some practical aspects of the problems involved. There is a wholesome relationship between the sexes, as brothers and sisters in the Lord, and in some cases, as spiritual mothers or fathers and sons or daughters, which is pleasing to our Heavenly Father. There is expressed in such fellowship a respect and an affection which produces true Christian friendship. There are also the more impersonal teacher-student, counselor-counselee, leader-follower, and even employer-employee relationships within the Christian community which involve necessary interaction between the sexes at various levels.

"It is not good that man should be alone" refers to more than just the intimate relationship of marriage. The experience of man is enhanced by the presence of mothers, sisters, and daughters in the Lord. His life will not be spiritually, psychologically, or socially complete without the ministry of God's handmaidens. The converse is true, of course, for our sisters in Christ. They likewise, need their spiritual fathers, brothers, and sons to fulfill their lives in God's family. Many beautiful illustrations of this truth are found in Scriptures—including the life of Jesus our Lord!

There is a uniqueness to the marriage relationship, encompassing but surpassing the above, which is ordained of God and should be guarded as most precious. It involves an intimate sharing together in life at every level: spiritually, psychologically (rationally and emotionally), physically, and socially. Marriage has been sanctified as a symbol of the personal relationship of every believer individually, and the Church corporately, with Christ as the Heavenly Bridegroom. It was designed to be the fountainhead of life from which mankind could fulfill the divine call of creation. The sexual function in marriage is elevated to a place of holy beauty and purpose as a unique sign of love and fidelity. No wonder the Deceiver seeks to defile the marriage relationship by extending its exclusive privileges beyond the bounds God Himself has established. In this way the uniqueness of spiritual purpose between partners in marriage is lost!

The Tempter achieves his evil endeavors in most beguiling ways. A Spirit-filled individual may have a mate whose interests are most indifferent or antagonistic to spiritual things. In the course of spiritual fellowship and even Christian witness a genuine affinity may develop for someone who seemingly possesses everything which is so obviously missing in one's partner at home. The relationship may progress no further than a fantasy of the heart and mind. A life is weakened, however, and an estrangement may develop with one's spouse that totally restrains the redeeming power of the Holy Spirit for the home. Such tendencies should be immediately renounced and the releasing power of the Holy Spirit confessed. The Lord cares and understands, but cannot bless a wandering heart. *To persist in such imaginations is to open our minds to outright delusion!*

I know of a lady who actually believed she should leave her husband and marry a man she felt was her true God-given "soul mate," a man with whom she could "flow together" in the Spirit. This was supposedly even confirmed by "prophecy." She was quite serious about the matter and believed this was the only way "her ministry" could really develop for God's glory. The only difficulty was that her soul mate turned out to be the local rector who was already happily married with a large family, and quite oblivious of her intentions!

Unfortunately, in some situations, warm overtures of friendship may be welcomed in the wrong way by a lonely and like-minded individual. What begins together as prayer over "mutual problems" can take on a soulish emphasis which is psychologically most overpowering, opening our lives to the deception of the Devil. Intimate physical expressions of love and sympathetic understanding may reach an erotic level. If the Holy Spirit's initial warning signals are ignored, the relationship can develop in such a beguiling way that an illicit love affair, for a time, may even seem to be a thing of beauty. *It is not so in God's eyes, and only tragedy and disappointment can be forecast for the future!*

In every case where such situations have fully developed God has endeavored at many points along the way to bring the discernment of the Spirit. Often this may even be followed by counsel and admonitions from godly leaders of the Christian community. When such warnings are willfully and persistently ignored, the heart and mind can be so deceived that, short of a deliverance, the individual can no longer be reached at all. *Delusion doesn't come overnight; it must be cultivated!*

As soon as any personal relationship develops that is at all questionable, God requires that we take immediate and decisive action. Jesus instructed His disciples along these lines by the illustration of the offending eye or hand. They were to be immediately removed. *We are not to slowly saw our way through, or cut something off inch by inch, but decisively disengage ourselves with one blow!*

I know of a Christian leader who felt a "soul mate" relationship had developed between his secretary and himself. He refused to remove his secretary and give God a chance to reorient his heart and mind concerning his family responsibilities. There is little opportunity for the Holy Spirit to bring clear discernment as long as delusion is being mutually reenforced by the parties involved.

If the reader feels the Holy Spirit is convicting him about a questionable relationship in his own life. *he should immediately disengage himself from the situation and seek prayer and assistance from a spiritual counselor.* Little light will be forthcoming as long as he remains involved and merely tries to figure it out for himself. "The heart is deceitful above all things" and cannot be trusted after we become intimately and emotionally involved in an unwholesome relationship. We need the detachment which only the Spirit can bring when we in faith have *come apart* and submitted ourselves to His faithful ministry. God is a Good Shepherd!

There is another kind of unhealthy relationship that needs to be recognized. It can develop in a situation where the husband is considered to be less godly minded than the wife. Consequently, she must find her spiritual fellowship and strength from other sources. This may include a special prayer-partner or a ladies' prayer group. Such encouragement is essential and to be greatly appreciated. An atmosphere of love and faith can restore our souls during times of discouragement and despair. I know of a saintly woman who, facing family problems herself, opened her home for wives who wanted to agree together that the Lord would heal their homes. Already God has worked some real miracles in their marriages, and they are united in prayer and purpose that the Holy Spirit will perfect all that He has begun in their midst.

Problems arise, however, where the fellowship or prayer-partner becomes a haven for sympathy and self-pity rather than redemptive prayer and spiritual counsel. This will only foster feelings of hostility and resentment toward one's mate and hinder the healing power God would bring to the home. *Furthermore, there can be an unwholesome transfer of confidence and even love from one's mate to the partner or group.* This need not be in any sexually perverted way, but the consequence is an alienation of affection which will result in spiritual, psychological, and even physical withdrawal from one's marriage partner.

All of this may be accomplished within the framework of something that is supposed to be "spiritual." There may even be mighty manifestations of the Spirit which would seem to confirm this tendency toward alienation, but nevertheless it is an abomination before the Lord. Usually this occurs where there is such an emphasis on "spiritual things" that it implies a withdrawal from such "earthly things" as nonspiritual husbands. This is a false sense of spirituality which is harsh and unlovely. It is in sharp contrast to the faith, hope, and love which characterizes true handmaidens of God.

HALF-TRUTH IS NOT THE WHOLE TRUTH

Many false prophets promote their error by presenting only a part of the truth, carefully avoiding the whole truth. I drove my wife to a ladies' prayer meeting one evening and was invited to remain and share with them. In the course of the meeting they played a religious tape from a weekly series to which they had subscribed.

A deep resonant voice suggested the listener find a comfortable chair and physically relax. One was then encouraged to come away from the cares and pressures of the weary world, and enter into the silence of His presence. Here divine truth and love would clear away confusion and pain and flood one's being with holy light from within.

I opened one eye and all the ladies were entering into "the rest" as prescribed. The soothing voice of the speaker would have been somewhat conducive to sleep had it not been for a strong sense of inner restlessness in my spirit. The words were peaceful enough, but something was wrong. I prayed that I might not be critical or jealous, but discerning and spiritually alert. After a while it became rather obvious that the divine presence, silence, rest, peace, light, and love of God was at no time centered in Jesus. His name had not been mentioned once!

When the tape was through, I brought this to the attention of the ladies but was quickly and emphatically assured the gentleman was a great man of God through whose life much love and healing had been expressed. With that I pursued my concern no further, rationalizing my uncertain feelings as a personal and cultural reaction to a different approach to spiritual things.

My wife had not responded either, I discovered afterward, and was somewhat disturbed by similar tapes which were played during the weeks that followed. Some of the ladies were seemingly quite mature in the Lord and our first reaction was to depreciate and doubt our discernment.

Some weeks later the gentleman in question was scheduled to speak in the area at a special conference. We were invited to attend and lead a prayer circle afterward. At first I was tempted to decline, but realized this was an opportunity to prove out one way or another the validity of our earlier judgment. The meeting began in a warm and worshipful way and soon was given to the speaker of the evening. He was dressed in the black garb of a monk with sandals on his feet and a tasseled rope about his waist. His speech was forceful, fluent, and most eloquent. Personally, he was most charismatic in character!

The opening prayer confessed that the Father's love was enveloping saint and sinner alike. I felt uneasy about the omission of Jesus as the unique and final expression of that love, but realized that this was perhaps taken for granted. There were references to faith as the way to realize God's truth in our lives, but it was more of a faith in faith than a focus in Christ. There was, however, an occasional reference to our Lord and Savior and I then felt perhaps I had misjudged the man. Other questionable but nondecisive comments were made and I remained as uncertain as I had been before. A friend of mine had taken a seat next to me and he seemed to be thoroughly blessed by every word.

As I was holding the entire situation before the Lord, I was impressed to check a reference in the Scriptures I thought I might use in the prayer circle to follow. As I did, I glanced further on in the chapter to read these rather startling words:

"You seem so gullible: you believe whatever anyone tells you even if he is preaching about another Jesus than the One we preach, or a different spirit than the Holy Spirit you received, or shows you a different way to be saved. You swallow it all ... God never sent these men at all; they are "phonies" who have fooled you into thinking they are Christ's apostles. Yet I am not surprised! Satan can change himself into an angel of light" (II Cor. 11:4, 13-14; *Living Letters*).

Then an unexpected thing happened. I saw a vision of a shining golden pole or shaft. Encircled around it, but not in actual contact with it, was a slender bright green serpent. It wasn't an ugly viper, but more like a graceful grass snake which is not only harmless but rather charming in appearance. (Some foreign snakes of this description are extremely deadly.) I recall raising the question in my mind, "What in the world does this mean?" Immediately there was an almost audible reply: *"Ever approaching but never touching the truth!"*

The kind of Jesus that Paul preached is our standard of Truth. Born of a virgin, the Son of God becomes the Son of man. He was the express image of God; He uniquely died for our sins and arose in resurrection power. He ascended to the right hand of the Father from whence He sent forth the Holy Spirit. He will come again as He left to judge both the living and the dead and thereby determine their destiny for heaven or hell. This is the Jesus that Paul preached! This was not the Jesus that was presented by the ministry in question.

This answered my questions, but the final confirmation came months later when some of the literature of his ministry came into my hands. I discarded the materials into the wastebasket, but felt impressed of God to retrieve it for purposes of examination. There in bold print was a denial of the unique power of Christ's shed blood for the remission of sins. Sin was not viewed as man's self-willed way in rebellion to God, but rather an error in thought which did not appreciate man's innate goodness. Salvation was defined as recognizing the truth concerning the divine flame of light and life within each man which awaits to be expressed as we submit to the royal law of love.

No need for the redemptive work of the cross; man can be his own Savior. If he fails to realize the truth here, he will experience it in heaven where God's life and love will be fully expressed. Judgment is experienced now and is the result of a life lived in error. There is, therefore, no need to prepare for a day of divine reckoning, and most certainly there is no place for hell in God's great heart of love.

Sounds great! *But, what a cruel fool it makes of our Heavenly Father for allowing His Son to die on the cross after He pleaded to be spared if there was another possible way for man to be redeemed.* What a mockery of God's grace! Such is the error that prevails when another Jesus other than Paul's Jesus is preached. When Jesus declared He was *the* way, *the* truth and *the* life, He really meant that He was the *only* way, the *whole* truth and life *everlasting.* Truly, there is no other way to the Father! Paul's Jesus is indeed a powerful standard against which we can measure truth and error.

THE MYSTERY OF BABYLON

"And upon her forehead was a name written, MYSTERY, BABYLON THE GREAT, THE MOTHER OF HARLOTS AND ABOMINATIONS OF THE EARTH" (Rev. 17:5). There is a spiritual mystery here which relates to the soulish tendency of man to interweave his own religious schemes into the spiritual fabric of the true Church. That which originates from the carnal mind (forehead) of man, however, is always in opposition to the Spirit although it may initially appear in a religious garb. It also paves the way for outright Satanic deception and delusion. In any case, such soulish conceptions are an abomination to the Lord and ultimately will be destroyed.

The word "Babylon" means "confusion" and historically refers to the confusion of tongues which came because of the erection of the Tower of Babel. The tower symbolizes man's arrogant attempt to "reach into the heavens" by his own efforts. It was designed by man, built by human hands, and totally earthy in its composition. While most appealing to the natural eye, it was an abomination to the Lord, for every brick was befouled by the sweat and smell of soulish endeavor. *Here was man's attempt to unify and dignify himself apart from God's purpose and power!* Instead of blessing, however, it brought a divine curse and confusion. So it is today wherever men substitute their soulish systems for the life, power, and divine order which only the Blessed Holy Spirit can produce.

Such earthly towers of men stand out in clear contrast to the beautiful Temple of God which is arising unassisted by human hands (Acts 7:48; Eph. 2:19-22). We are the living stones of His workmanship finding our place in His Temple by divine appointment (I Pet. 2:4-5).

All other constructions produce only pride, suspicion, and division among the members of the Father's family! The spirit of Babylon always produces a strong sectarian attitude in the lives of those possessed and thereby inflicts wounds within the Body of Christ. No wonder the Scriptures exhort God's people to "Come out of her . . . that ye be not partakers of her sins, and that ye receive not of her plagues" (Rev. 18:4).

Basically and initially, "coming out of Babylon" is an inner change of heart which shifts one's loyalty from an earthly framework with its man-made fences to the true vision of the Church which the Holy Spirit is universally revealing to those who have been Spirit-baptized by Jesus Christ. Real charismatic communities become fountainheads of resurrection life for the dead, dry bones of Christendom long since buried in the sterile traditions of men (Ezek. 37:1-14). Perhaps this is one of the "greater works" Jesus promised we would do after He ascended to the Father! (John 14:12).

Some equate all "organized churches" as synonymous with "Babylon." That the spirit of Babylon is manifested in some denominational systems is not to be denied. It is also found, however, in "non-denominational" fellowships and even in informal church-in-the-home groups. *It is one thing to take "people out of Babylon" and another thing to take "Babylon out of the people"!* Many local groups have succeeded only in building their own little towers related to doctrine, patterns of worship, and governmental control. Each considers itself to be the true expression of "the local New Testament Church" and often will recognize no other assembly as really "legitimate." Such an exclusive attitude is denying the very basis for true fellowship in Jesus.

One is impressed with the Apostle Paul's exhortation concerning division in the body of Christ as expressed in I Corinthians 1:10-17. The Corinthians were basing their fellowship around men. Paul indicates that all were in error, even those who boasted they were of Christ, because of their exclusive attitude. No one would recognize the other, and division was the result.

There are some subtle forms of deception which are related to this kind of division. *The groups involved usually emphasize obedience to those in positions of local authority above the responsibility of the individual to the Lordship of Jesus personally!* As a result, homes and families have been split and a legal, loveless attitude develops. The strong dominating power of such groups may be hidden until a difference of opinion concerning spiritual things is raised. Great emphasis is placed on personal submission to the ruling elders or "body" as a whole. This is enforced by intimidation. To disobey is to invoke God's wrath! Because there is much apparent blessing and truth in many respects, one can fearfully question the discernment the Spirit of truth is actually revealing to them. I have counseled with many confused and frightened people who have been hurt and scarred by such misguided ministries. It is beautiful to see Jesus heal and set them free!

The Holy Spirit is going to be shaking, sifting, all of Christendom at every level in these days before us. This includes our own lives and Christian communities as well as others who we have always felt should be shaken. (We would even help the Lord out when it comes to the others!) At the same time we are going to be surprised to see God's Spirit moving in places which perhaps many of us thought were out of bounds. Somehow the Holy Spirit can move into some of the "strangest places" to reach searching souls and hungry hearts.

Sometimes the Lord leads individuals out of their local situations; other times He leaves them in as "missionaries" to their own people. The demoniac of Gadara, after his deliverance, requested that he might leave the area which had been so unreceptive to Jesus and follow Him as a disciple. The Lord wisely refused, but rather told him to go home to his people and share the goodness and love of God with them. He obeyed and was able to present a witness in an area that wouldn't have accepted Christ in person! (Luke 5:1-20). *We may not be able to change "the establishment," but we can bring the life and love of Jesus to those whom God has prepared us to serve!*

Furthermore, if one's church is truly Christ-centered and Bible-oriented, there is a stability and safety which such fellowship can afford as one matures in his newfound walk in the Spirit. There is much to learn from all of our brothers and sisters, even those who may not presently understand the charismatic renewal in the churches. Many of them have moved further out into the stream of the Spirit in some areas than we have fully realized. In some situations, we need them as much as they need us in God's overall view. We must ever guard against pride and be as humble and honest as we know how in the Lord.

Not every pastor in the "organized church" is an example of the "blind leading the blind." Many accept their responsibility as under-shepherds with utmost sincerity and are concerned for the immature and even obstinate sheep within the fold. *Love is patient and long-suffering as Jesus was with His disciples!* Even Judas was treated with understanding until his decision against the Lord was finalized and he separated himself from the fellowship of the disciples. Wherever possible may we bring blessing rather than confusion and division.

The seeds of love and truth grow quietly but most irresistibly, if God has prepared the soil. The "gifts" must be set in the "graces"! The gifts were designed to be clothed in the fruit of the Spirit to be fully effective in God's glorious purpose for His people. The best testing and proving ground for God's work in our lives is often the very setting in which we were placed when we met Jesus Christ as the Baptizer. Some of the finest and most beautiful fruit of the Spirit is grown in just that kind of soil. A hasty spirit has probably limited God's witness more times and in more ways than we realize. I know my wife and I have always felt we were premature in resigning so soon from our local church following our blessing in the fullness of God's Holy Spirit. We never really gave the Lord the time He needed in expressing to others the new life of joy and freedom we had discovered in meeting Jesus as our Blessed Baptizer. Perhaps others can profit from our mistake. *We are responsible for discerning not only God's will and His way, but also His timing!*

Babylon represents the soulish schemes of man which substitute worldly traditions for the direction and power of the Holy Spirit, and it is also the fountainhead for outright Satanic delusion and deception. As mentioned before, he will often appear as an angel of light within a "spiritual" or even "religious" context. The Scriptures clearly define and emphatically renounce all such devilish deceptions:

"Keep to your spells then and all your sorceries, for which you have worn yourself out since your youth. Do you think they will help you? Do you think they will make anyone nervous? You have spent weary hours with your many advisers. Let them come forward now and save you, these who analyse the heavens, who study the stars and announce month by month what will happen to you next.

"Oh, they will be like wisps of straw and the fire will burn them. They will not save their lives from the power of the flame. No embers these, for baking, no fireside to sit by. This is what your wizards will be for you, those men for whom you have worn yourself out since your youth. They will all go off, each his own way, powerless to save you" (Isa. 47:12-15, *New Jerusalem Bible*).

"When you come into the land which the Lord your God gives you, you shall not learn to follow the abominable practices of these nations. There shall not be found among you any one who makes his son or daughter pass through the fire, or who uses divination, or is a soothsayer, or an augur, or a sorcerer, or a charmer, or a medium, or a wizard, or a necromancer.

"For all who do these things are an abomination to the Lord; and it is because of these abominable practices that the Lord your God is driving them out from before you. You shall be blameless (and absolutely true) to the Lord your God. For these nations, whom you shall dispossess, listen to soothsayers and diviners, but as for you, the Lord your God has not allowed you to do so" (Deut. 18:9-14, *Amplified Bible*).

Other related passages include: Exod. 22:18; Lev. 19:26,31; 20:6, 27; Deut. 4:19; 13:1-5, 17:2-5; II Kings 9:22; 17:16-17; 21:2-6; 23:24; I Chron. 10:13-14; Isa. 8:19; 47:9, 12-14; Jer. 8:1-2; 14:14; 19:13; 27:9-10; 29:8-9; Zeph. 1:4-6; Acts 16:16-18; 19:19; Gal. 3:1-3; 4:10-11; 5:19-21; Rev. 9:20-21; 18:23; 21:8; 22:14-15.

Sorcery refers to the practice of the occult arts under the power of evil spirits. In modern language such practices include: fortune-telling, palm reading, card reading, Ouija Board, seances, spiritism, development of extrasensory powers (ESP), hypnotism, spirit writing, water witching, psychometry, black and white magic, astrology, yoga, and other mystic cults. To personally and directly explore any of these areas even out of curiosity can lead to serious Satanic oppression. Not everyone with such experiences in his background has been so influenced, but many have, as the author can confirm from personal counseling experience.

The Scriptures repeatedly denounce and warn against involvement in any form with the above activities, as harmless as some of them may seem on the surface. (There is a rash of parlor games designed to test one's extrasensory powers.) In the Old Testament economy, violators were sometimes stoned, so serious were such offenses before the Lord (Lev. 20:6, 27). In the New Testament we are clearly informed that all sorcerers (practitioners of the occult) will find their part in the lake of fire (Rev. 21:8).

Even Spirit-baptized Christians have been deceived into pursuing one area or another without realizing the related danger. Astrology can be presented in a beguiling way as a spiritual blessing which has been ordained of God to enhance man's welfare. *This is a lie, and to willfully submit to what God has cursed will lead ultimately to spiritual darkness and delusion!*

Perhaps the reader has not been aware of the seriousness involved in such activities up to this point. The Lord stands ready to forgive and release you from the influence of such relationships in the past. The prayer for deliverance earlier in this chapter covers just such areas as here described. *God requires only a deliberate renouncement of all such activity on your part and a confession of Christ's releasing power!* He is the Lord of our lives, and as our Good Shepherd His protection and guidance is assured both now and for these important days before us.

DEMONISM

There are those who scoff at the reality of Satan as a personal intelligence with a host of evil spirits (demons) to assist him in his opposition to God's will here on earth. *There are so many references to the Devil and his demons in the Bible that to deny their existence would be to deny the personality of Christ and the holy angels, if we wanted to be logically consistent.* Obviously Satan would not have us take his kingdom seriously in any personal sense since this would lead to real Christians taking up their armor and engaging him in spiritual conflict (Eph. 6:10-18).

Many relegate demonic activity only to Bible history and deny the influence of demons in modern times. Others believe their power is experienced only in primitive cultures as evidenced by stories from missionaries. With the rapid increase of evil in our own country, however, more are ready to believe something is behind perversion and atrocity. Still some may not realize that demonic oppression of Spirit-baptized saints is possible, and blame everything but the real enemy for their affliction. Obviously relief is forthcoming. *God is restoring a sound, wholesome ministry of deliverance to the body of Christ.* He wants His people free to move forth in the full force and power of His Holy Spirit. There is nothing more beautiful than to see individual lives not only being released from the hold of the Enemy, but then ministering deliverance to others who have been bound by Satan's power.

Not every problem in life is demonic in origin. Satan in his cunning way would deceive us into embracing error by starting with the truth and then taking us beyond its limit. If we cannot be misled into denying or ignoring demonic power, the Devil will entice us into becoming preoccupied with it. *Some people spend more time confessing demons than they do the Lord!* They assign every adverse circumstance to demonic activity. Every weakness of the flesh, in themselves and others, is viewed as the direct result of demonic influence. As a result, they become fearful and suspicious and unknowingly cast a spiritual shadow upon all whom they encounter. The Enemy revels in such attention and praise.

Others, instead of becoming fearful, develop a very proud and critical spirit as they analyze every problem and every person in terms of demonic power. They become self-styled "deliverers" who, by virtue of their strong personalities, intimidate more sensitive individuals who submit to their ministries out of fear. I heard of one person who was "turned over to the tormentors" because he refused to "cooperate" in a prayer for deliverance. The story was finally shared with the person's Spirit-filled pastor who immediately released the individual in Jesus' name from her fear and anxiety. Such episodes cast shadows on genuine ministries of deliverance which are usually very balanced in their character.

The true test of a wholesome, balanced ministry is the "life" that is forthcoming in the Christian community as a whole after it leaves! If division, confusion, and uncertainty are the results, something is out of divine order. This does not mean there may not be some blessing and even many supernatural manifestations of the Spirit, but the real test is still the healing life of Jesus for His entire body.

As mentioned before, true deliverance involves spiritually discerning the problem both in terms of *source* and the *method* or means God would choose to bring a release. We live in a sin-cursed world and are subjected to the downward pull of our soulish natures apart from the Holy Spirit. The disorder, ugliness, pain, and death which is a part of our natural world is Satanic in origin but not necessarily demonic in expression. There are not thistle and thorn demons or hurricane demons, but both are manifestations of a creation which waiteth for its redemption (Rom. 8:19-23).

This is not to deny the possibility of direct, demonic activity involving natural phenomena in some cases. I have always felt the storms on the sea of Galilee which threatened the life of our Lord and His disciples may have been more than just meteorological disturbances. Generally speaking, however, most natural distresses can hardly be designated as demonic in origin. Nor is the Christian immune from all such natural disorders. *Where not protected, however, we are perfected, for God will work all things together for the good purpose of conforming us into His image! (Rom. 8:28-29).*

Likewise, the works of the flesh are expressions of our carnal natures and not always direct evidences of demonic activity (Gal. 5:19-21). To knowingly and persistently yield to such weaknesses of the flesh or to indulge in excesses of anything which weakens us spiritually or physically is, however, an open invitation in some cases to demonic influence. *What begins under our control leads us into a subjection which is overpowering!* In such situations, only the power of Jesus can set the person free.

Some people, in blaming demons for everything, fail to see they are avoiding their responsiblity to face themselves before the Lord. It is easier to obtain "instant holiness" through an exorcism that it is to submit daily to the sanctifying power of the Holy Spirit that we might take up our cross and follow Jesus. *The prayer-chair of deliverance can never substitute for the day-by-day ministry of the cross in our lives!*

Where genuine demonic influence is limiting a life, God wants to express His love by releasing that life completely to His Son. Some individuals are so bound they may have almost lost the will to the power of the Enemy. God can set them free by the prayer of faith and the authority of Jesus' name. *Such a release, however, can be maintained only if they choose to remain free!* Some individuals enjoy communion with spirits that feed on their fleshly appetites. Some enjoy the attention or pity which their condition evokes from others and don't really want to be free.

I prayed twice for a lady who put on a spectacular dramatic display of demonic power and control. The first time I sensed a desire for show and attention and after prayer warned her never again to give in to this soulish desire for recognition. She was actually attracting and feeding demon powers which were most willing to gratify her desires. The second time she tried the same thing, I was unaware it was the same person. She was writhing around on the floor and the whole Bible class was rebuking all kinds of spirits as she identified them. This went on for some time, until I finally recognized who she was.

I dismissed the class except for a few ladies and sharply told her to get up and conduct herself in a seemly fashion. She obeyed with some reluctance and I could discern the Deceiver was trying to bluff his way out of the situation. I explained we would be pleased to decisively pray for her full release if she would repent of her desire to yield to the spirit of self-attention. *The next step was not prayer, but repentance!* She stubbornly refused. The Spirit had pierced through her phony display and revealed the intent of her heart, but she would not repent of her sin. She didn't want to be delivered. She thoroughly enjoyed her "deliverance sessions."

Many times God requires a person to cooperate in his own release. I shared for some time one afternoon with a student who was really bound spiritually and psychologically when she first arrived. As we shared together around the Lord, God's truth was progressively setting her free and she became more relaxed. Finally, only one chain remained and this related to her willingness to submit to the Spirit of praise which at one time had beautifully graced her life. Instead of sovereignly releasing her from the heavy hold of the Enemy, in this area, God gave her the key and required she unlock the chain herself as an expression of faith and obedience. She did after some wavering between the voice of God and that of the Devil, and she immediately found the freedom she sought.

A young woman who was tormented by timidity which limited her spiritual ministry in song requested prayer for deliverance. But instead of prayer, it was suggested she resist the Enemy herself in the name of Jesus. Demon powers can be weakened by refusing to give them the attention they thrive upon. They feed upon our fears and self-directed thoughts. Our power to resist and overcome increases as we feed upon God's truth and give attention to His Son by much praise and worship. Our faith becomes strong by praying in the Spirit and actively sharing His life and love with others. She was wisely encouraged to minister from time to time, and finally she found joy in actually offering to sing for God's glory. She progressively found real liberty and power in her ministry for the Lord.

The principles involved were clearly confirmed by a vision she received from the Lord. She saw what had been a great, black gorilla chained in her backyard. The creature was dead; nothing remained but a mass of hide and bones. The once powerful creature had been *starved* to death!

The Lord is revealing to His people the various ways by which the Holy Spirit can bring release to those who are oppressed by the Enemy. *Many have been set free by the power of God's Word alone!* I recall sharing in a Bible class the account of the lady referred to earlier in this chapter who was bound by fear but released as we prayed the Holy Spirit would move through her past life in healing power. All at once a lady in the audience began to laugh in an almost uncontrollable way. She had just been gloriously set free herself as she had listened in faith to this story of God's liberating power. This has happened many times through the ministry of the Word without any formal prayer being offered. I have claimed that many who are reading this chapter will experience God's liberating power in their own lives by confessing their own deliverance. Often only two people are really required for such an experience—you and the Lord!

Sometimes in Spiritual Life classes we have analyzed the cause and consequences of fear which Satan would exploit in our lives. The first time I shared along these lines the Lord brought a change in presentation I hadn't planned on. God prompted the class to share their fears and the fruit such fears produced. People shared things never before admitted, only to find others were plagued in the same way. It was interesting to see the common patterns that the Devil uses in oppressing God's people. *Often he deceives us into thinking nobody else has our kind of fears!* If we believe our problem is unique, we will question if we can really be helped. For instance, usually some fifty percent of each class questioned has felt at one time or another they had crossed God's line of grace by committing the unpardonable sin! (Incidently, if one had so grieved the Holy Spirit his conscience would be so seared he would have no concern whatsoever about spiritual things, including his eternal destiny.)

Here are some of the objects of fear which demon powers would magnify into dark clouds of oppression: death, sickness (as cancer), failure, criticism, rejection, ridicule, future, war, mental breakdown, old age, financial distress, accidents, natural catastrophes, loneliness, responsibility, unpardonable sin, second coming of Jesus, eternal judgment, decision, missing God's will, witnessing, praying aloud, and the phobias (dark, high places, people, crowds, water, animals, etc.). Do any of them sound familiar?

The following consequences of fear are listed as they too were presented by class members: depression, discouragement, anxiety, confusion, frustration, tension, weakness, self-pity, melancholy, introversion, self-depreciation, bitterness, anger, isolation, procrastination, indecision, irrational behavior, etc. No wonder the Scriptures declare "fear has torment" (I John 4:18).

The Son of God has been manifested that He might destroy these works of the Devil (I John 3:8). "The thief cometh not, but for to steal, and to kill, and to destroy: I am come that they might have life, and that they might have it more abundantly" (John 10:10). The Scriptures declare that we can overcome the Adversary because, "Greater is he that is in you than he that is in the world" (I John 4:4). This same indwelling Christ has assured us that He has given us power to tread on serpents and scorpions (demon powers), and over all the power of the Enemy: and nothing shall by any means hurt us! (Luke 10:19). If we first submit to God's Son, God's Spirit, and God's Word, we can resist the Devil and He will flee from us (Jas. 4:7). *You can overcome Satan now by the blood of the Lamb and the word of your testimony! (Rev. 12:11).*

Each oppressed person is a different situation, and the discernment of the Lord is is necessary to determine God's chosen way of release. *To rely upon a given method or formula is to invite disappointment and confusion!* Sometimes the Lord will supernaturally reveal the root of the problem which has given the Enemy his power over a life. It may be an attitude (resentment), a wound inflicted in early life (a specific incident), or a suppressed feeling of guilt that God wants brought to a place of conscious recognition in the light of His healing power.

Sometimes it is necessary for the person to share at length as the Spirit clears his life through the healing of his own spoken word before the Lord. At other times such sharing gives the listener spiritual insight into both the basic problem and God's answer. Many surface problems are only symptoms of, or even smoke screens for, the basic need. On some occasions what is needed is the ministry of God's Word followed by intercessory prayer.

In other situations, discussion would be utterly fruitless and only a decisive prayer for deliverance can open the mind darkened by delusion. A direct command to the demonic spirit to leave in Jesus' name can bring immediate relief. Stubborn cases may involve prayer and fasting and the ministry of several agreeing over a period of some time. More than one session may be required. I have seen God work in stages in some lives that had been deeply involved with evil powers. Deliverance may or may not be accompanied by physical manifestations (coughing, spitting, convulsions, or vocal outbursts). It is not wise to encourage such responses, but one can quickly explain should such things occur and questions arise.

At this point in my experience I think discretion should be used in presenting the message of deliverance with the intention of mass exorcism. People can be brought psychologically to a place of fear which is not the conviction of the Holy Spirit at all and leads to confusion and unnecessary distress. To encourage coughing and spitting during the process can also create an opportunity for the Enemy to magnify his presence. *There is a fine line between the power of suggestion, which is of man, and the power of conviction, which is of God!*

I have heard people confess to being delivered from the spirit of pride when I had the uneasy feeling they had been coerced by psychologically induced fear to request deliverance from a demon when the real answer was the work of the cross! A girl once almost glibly requested I pray for her "deliverance" as she was familiar with this ministry of exorcising demons. I didn't sense anything of a spiritual nature such as this and should not have even prayed. I did pray a general prayer for her release to Jesus and she immediately responded dutifully by coughing and announced she felt much better. The whole thing was psychological!

I have on many occasions, however, sensed a real spiritual power was oppressing one of God's saints and a sharp command in the name of Jesus brought an immediate release from tension, depression, pain, etc., followed by joy and relief. One lady with suicidal tendencies did respond by coughing but most have not. *I have the feeling that if the Enemy cannot keep God's people from a genuine deliverance ministry he will endeavor to exploit it in a way which exaggerates his power and leaves confusion, fear, and a preoccupation with demons!* This is often followed by a rash of self-styled deliverance ministries which actually exalt the Devil more than the Lordship of our Christ.

This has been of genuine concern to me for deliverance is a ministry which is desperately needed in the body of Christ. *The casting out of demons is as much a ministry of the church as is salvation and healing!* (Mark 16:15-20). It certainly characterized the apostolic age and needs a wholesome and proper emphasis for our day. Satan is moving with great power and wrath for "he knoweth he hath but a short time" (Rev. 12:12). This ministry will become increasingly important as the evil of our hour increases. It is apparent on every hand!

CONCLUSION

Let us pray that God will give His wisdom that the Enemy cannot pervert God's purpose in setting His people free. *The Devil's tactics have always been to so depreciate God's gifts in the hands of man, through misuse and abuse, that they will be brought to total disuse!* This has been true in all of the manifestations of God's Spirit which are evident expressions of His power: tongues, healings, miracles, etc. May we be bold for God but in a wise and understanding way that His full purpose in all of the gifts of the Spirit will be forthcoming.

May we also reaffirm God's desire that through His Spirit we may truly learn to be ourselves in Christ Jesus and thereby freely express His life to others. The Lord Himself releases us from the errors of the past and beckons us to arise and come away with Him. *God wants us to know we are free to follow His Son, for we will never respond to a freedom we don't believe we have!*

I was interested in the newspaper account of the African animals that were shipped to the West Coast recently to populate a newly developed wildlife entertainment center. When the cages were opened, some of the animals bounded out into the freedom of their new home without hesitation. Others remained within the confines of their little cramped cages and actually had to be prodded out into the open fields. Both groups of animals were released when the doors of the cages were opened. Only one group accepted their freedom and responded accordingly. The other group had been so conditioned by their long confinement they could not accept the freedom they were intended to have. They likewise responded accordingly!

The Song of Solomon (2:8-13) beautifully pictures for the Christian the invitation of our Beloved Bridegroom to experience the freedom in life which only His Spirit can bring to our longing hearts:

"The voice of my beloved! behold, he cometh leaping upon the mountains, skipping upon the hills.

"My beloved is like a roe or a young hart: behold he standeth behind our wall, he looketh forth at the windows, shewing himself through the lattice.

"My beloved spake, and said unto me, Rise up, my love, my fair one, and come away. For lo, the winter is past, the rain is over and gone;

"The flowers appear on the earth; the time of the singing of birds is come, and the voice of the turtle is heard in our land;

"The fig tree putteth forth her green figs, and the vines with the tender grape give a good smell. Arise, my love, my fair one, and come away."

To be filled with the Spirit is to be filled with the Truth that sets and keeps us free!

The Spirit of Holiness

The Greek word for holiness is "hagios." From the same root come the related English words, "sanctification" and "saint." The corresponding root word in Hebrew is "gadash." The range of meaning in English is found in the verbs: *dedicate, consecrate, sanctify, hallow, venerate, cleanse, purify, and perfect.*

To many people holiness and sanctification are practically synonymous with a narrow, gloomy, joyless type of existence. They tend to equate a holy life with a hollow life. Nothing could be further from the truth, and how Satan would desire to perpetuate this lie. To see clearly the blind and blurred areas in our understanding of true holiness, we must first look to Jesus and see the whole matter as related to Him. *The heavenly pattern of holiness for the earthly saint is found in God's Son.* He alone is *the* Holy One. Let us see what this means to us personally.

OUR CALLING AND OUR CONDUCT

The Apostle Peter relates the holy life to our *call* and to our *conduct.* "Like obedient children, do not shape your lives by the cravings which were formerly yours in the time of your ignorance, but, in imitation of the Holy One who has called you, do you also be holy in all your behavior, since it is written, 'you are to be holy, because I am holy' " (I Pet. 1:14-16 Weymouth).

One morning some time ago when we were living on the West Coast, I was driving to school for my morning classes. On the way I passed the elementary school where our children were then enrolled. As I approached I heard a loud bell persistently and repeatedly ringing. At first I wondered what such an unusual sound at that hour of the day might mean. It then occurred to me that it was probably the fire bell for a safety drill. In a moment I would be turning the corner of the school and the playgrounds would be in view where the children assembled during such practice sessions.

As I looked back, I saw the doors of the school open wide and hundreds of children rapidly make their way to their appointed places of safety. Everyone was assembling as had been previously planned. The purpose of the ringing bell was now most obvious—for them it was a lifesaving sound!

I began to respond to the experience in a rather unusual way as I drove on past the school. Tears came to my eyes and I was most moved within. True, my children were among those whom I had seen, but my emotional response was far beyond what one would normally expect. It was then that I realized that God was trying to speak to me. As I submitted to the Spirit of prophecy, the message came forth as if God Himself were speaking:

"My son, I, too, am calling, loudly and persistently that the saints might hear my voice and quickly respond. I desire that in the coming hour of danger they might assemble themselves together as the hour approaches. For yet a little while, and the yoke of the Enemy shall be destroyed by the anointing (Holy Spirit) that will rest upon their lives."

The word "saint" means a *called-out-one*. The primary requisite for sainthood is to hear the call of Christ and respond to His claims upon our lives. "My sheep *hear* my voice . . . and they *follow* me" (John 10:27). This is the simple twofold basis for the life of holiness. *To hear and to follow speaks of our calling and our conduct.*

JESUS IS OUR HOLY PATTERN

The door and the way to the saintly life is both straight and narrow. "Strait is the gate, and narrow is the way, which leadeth unto life" (Matt. 7:14). Note this passage is not referring so much to *a way of life* as it is to *the way to life.* Jesus is simultaneously the door, the way, and the life. He said so! "I am the Door. Anyone who enters in through Me will be saved—will live" (John 10:9 *Amplified Bible*). "I am the Way and the Truth and the Life; no one comes to the Father except by (through) Me" (John 14:6 *Amplified Bible*). There is only *one* true door, *one* true way, and *one* true life! The Bible narrows the range of possibilities by which we can find the true life of holiness to one; that one possibility is a person, and that person is Jesus Christ. The life of holiness is the life that Christ is. "Be ye holy for I am holy." *Sanctification is the process by which the Holy Spirit conforms us into the holy image of God's Son!*

The twofold pattern of calling and conduct is beautifully illustrated for us in the life of Christ. Jesus was a marked man from his birth. He was called to be the Savior of the world. Even the name Jesus Christ in the original languages refers to His Saviorhood and Messiahship. He was called to be a man of destiny. His life was lived with a divine sense of mission and purpose. Every minute of His life was meaningful. Every encounter He had with people was divinely ordered. Every circumstance of His life was charged with eternal significance. Everything pointed in one divine direction. His only desire and great delight was to fulfill the will of His Father. He set His face like a flint and allowed nothing to swerve Him from fulfilling His divine destiny.

The conduct of His life reflected the commitment of His soul. There was a discipline to each day which was related to the direction of His life. His motives were pure. His life was clean. His heart was perfect. He was moved with compassion but was never mastered by feeling. Communication with the Father was constantly clear. His life was perfectly transparent and never once was it clouded with the sin of selfishness. The eternal purposes of heaven were ever so real that the temporal pleasures of the world never possessed His life. He was *in* the world but not *of* the world. He hated sin but loved the sinner. He sat with sinners but was never soiled by their sin. To touch His life at any time or in any place or with any one was to touch the holiness of God. Indeed He was the sinless Son of God. *Jesus Christ was absolutely and altogether holy!*

THE HOLY SPIRIT: OUR PURIFYING POWER

With great feeling we now respond to our Lord's clear call to us, "Be ye holy, for I am holy." We are both amazed and humbled at such a high and holy calling. *As sons of God we, too, have become marked men and women from the day of our spiritual birth!* And as fantastic as it seems, our Lord emphatically declares that as the Father sent Him, so sends He us to live a holy life in a most unholy world. The implications of our calling can be as frustrating and discouraging as they are amazing until we realize it is going to be accomplished in His way, not ours.

Once again we are directed to the third Person of the Trinity. He is God's way to personal holiness. As His name implies, He is the very Spirit of holiness. *It is His ministry to progressively reveal and release the holiness of Christ in and through our lives!* An Episcopalian friend rather vividly expressed it this way: "After I was filled with the Holy Spirit, I soon discovered that He was just waiting to take His little broom and begin housecleaning.'

As the light of God's Spirit shines fully into our lives, a lifetime accumulation of trash, dust, and cobwebs comes to our attention and His. He requests permission to clean up one area of our life after another. If given free reign, He works with amazing swiftness and most efficiently. His housecleaning tools are varied and some are most unusual. In fact, at the time we may never even recognize them as such. It is only after all is done that we realize that another room has become clean and bright.

We never readily appreciate how many rooms, closets, and cupboards there are in these earthly temples of ours until God begins His work of cleansing. Some areas are so easily and quickly brightened up that we aren't even aware of the change until some time later. Then to our surprise we notice that some musty corner of our life that had been a little dark and dingy before is now fresh and clean. Other areas seem to require rather persistent scrubbing and, to our dismay, are easily soiled again. However, by quickly submitting to the purifying power of God's forgiving Spirit as soon as the stains of sin are discovered, we find even these parts of our lives becoming shining examples of God's perfecting power.

Occasionally the Holy Spirit will come to a closet in these lives of ours which is closed to His presence. Knowing that Jesus can never be completely at home in a life where forbidden areas remain, He kindly but insistently asks us for the key. To resist His persistent plea brings conflict and confusion into our lives. We quickly realize that we are facing a far greater issue than the particular one with which the Holy Spirit confronts us. The real issue centers in our professed Lordship of Jesus Christ. If we are not completely mastered by Jesus Christ, then He is not really Master at all for us! *The Holy Spirit's deep desire for you and me is that Christ Jesus be Lord of all . . . all of you and all of me!*

HOLINESS IS A LOVE RELATIONSHIP

True holiness can never be cataloged as a list of do's and don'ts. *Rather holiness is an attitude of heart that lovingly recognizes the Lordship of Jesus Christ!* We become willing bondslaves of our loving Lord. We are as committed to Him through the bonds of love as He is committed to the will of the Father.

Real holiness is a love relationship! A wedding ring is a seal and a symbol of eternal and undivided love. It is a love gift from the groom to the bride. The Spirit of Holiness is Christ's love gift to His Bride. It is the seal of our holy union with Him in salvation. It was a costly gift, and Jesus paid the full price. He gave Himself, all of Himself, that we through the Holy Spirit might intimately and personally know the life and love of God. Jesus was utterly and completely broken that we might have unbroken communion with Him.

It all becomes so clear in the light of God's love. *Holiness is Calvary!* It is an all-out surrender to the love and will of God, that His life might find full expression through ours. How trite and trivial is the attitude that tries to calculate how far one can go without being labeled "worldly."

So often we have a tendency to logically construct an artificial list of worldly do's and don't's as if holiness of heart could be measured by men's minds. God's standard of holiness so far transcends any yardstick that we might project that we would do better to look first to His Son before looking to the world. It is possible to become so possessed by the negative attitude of avoiding the world that we almost become more worldly minded than the sinner who unconsciously is a part of it. How much better to be so possessed by the love of Jesus Christ that we always aim to order our behavior in such a way as to continually promote His presence in our lives and the lives of others. He then becomes our standard of holiness. *The more His measure increases in our lives the more wholesomely holy do we naturally become.*

To be wedded to God's Son speaks of a life of holy adventure! We have dedicated ourselves to the exciting purpose of knowing Him and sharing Him with others. We jealously guard against anything that would so possess our body, mind, or spirit that our daily communion with Him or witness for Him might become clouded or confused. This is a most exacting but divinely exhilarating way to live. This is life as it was meant to be!

A truly holy life is also a very lovely life! It is a life in which nothing detracts from the beauty of the indwelling Christ. Just as we would never display a magnificent work of art in a cheap, gaudy picture frame, so our lives must suitably frame the lovely portrait of our Lord. The sensitive Christian will be very careful concerning extremes in conversation, conduct, or dress. Our desire is to allow our lives to become an attractive setting for His presence.

The principles which we have just shared together have very practical, present-tense applications. As we yield our total being to the Holy Spirit, He will faithfully and progressively deal with various dimensions of our lives which need His sanctifying touch. To realize that God desires to freshen and cleanse new areas of our lives each day lends a holy excitement to our Christian experience. He doesn't always begin at the same place in each life, and we must be careful not to gauge the spiritual progress of others by the precise way in which He is working in ours. God begins where we are and with the areas of greatest need. Let us allow Him to do His work in His way in our lives and in the lives of others. If we continue to encourage one another in the Spirit, He will faithfully proceed with His perfecting work.

What we think, say, and do; where we go; what we listen to and look at; how we budget our time and order our lives; even how we care for our physical bodies will all come under the silent scrutiny of God's Holy Spirit. With expectation we will listen to hear what suggestions He will make and how He will enable us to meet the challenge of the disciplined life.

We will soon discover that there may be some things that others can do that we cannot! We will be careful, however, not to judge others remembering the converse is also true. Also, many things that now seem to be such a permanent part of our life may strangely lose their importance as better things take their place. God will continually be leading us from the harmful to the good, to the better, to the best. At each step we find new freedom and wonder why we previously were so attached to unessentials.

HOLINESS IS A PURIFYING HOPE

The theme of personal holiness takes on a timely significance when we see it related to the character of the Church just prior to our Lord's return. Paul shares with us the desires of the Heavenly Bridegroom that His Bride, the Church, should be sanctified, cleansed, and washed. In fact, she is to be presented as a glorious Church without blemish (Eph.

116

5:26-27).

The end-time Church is also going to be characterized as a militant church. She will be consecrated for the purpose of a great worldwide witness unto all the nations. "... then shall the end come" (Matt. 24:14). This twofold character of *purity* and *power* will be the result of the *sanctifying* and *unifying* work of the Holy Spirit who in these last days is being poured out upon all flesh.

As individual members of the Church, we should relate our lives to the lateness of the hour in a meaningful way. The secular world is certainly aware of the uniqueness of our atomic age. *The Bulletin of the Atomic Scientists* is a publication which is dedicated to the peculiar problems of our times. On the cover of every issue is the face of a clock, the hands of which are set at five minutes to twelve. No one knows when the clock may strike, but there is an awareness that time may be shorter than we think. The newspaper headlines daily reinforce this feeling of uneasiness.

As Christians we are told that when the signs of the end-time begin to appear, we are to look up for our redemption draweth nigh. In other words, we are to lift our heads and be alert and allow the second coming of Christ to be a *purifying hope* which quickens our desire to redeem the time and live life with eternity in full view. Perhaps we need to feel the same sense of commitment to God's holy will as Jesus did when He realized His hour was fast approaching. *Our hour may be closer upon us than we realize!*

What a motivating and purifying hope the soon return of the Lord becomes to our daily lives. The Holy Scriptures would even indicate that we can hasten the day of His appearance by keeping our lives filled with His Spirit of purity and power. As we encourage others to be continually filled with God's Spirit, we are actually playing a necessary part in preparing the Bride of Christ for her Bridegroom! Surely in view of our times we can make Peter's admonition our daily prayer. "What manner of persons ought [we] to be in all holy conversation and godliness, Looking for and hastening unto the coming of the day of God ..." (II Pet. 3:11-12).

THE URGENCY OF OUR HOUR

Recently my wife and I prayed that God would confirm the sense of urgency in our lives which we have associated with the soon return of our Lord. I felt almost compelled to request that God would answer our prayer within the week if it were His will. The next morning I received a letter in the mail from an attorney in Los Angeles who has recently been filled with God's Spirit. The Lord had awakened him at 12:25 a.m. a few days previously, and the Holy Spirit had given him the following prophecy:

"Now we must all work together in the Spirit. Call on each dear brother as the need arises. Tell your problems freely. Ask for counsel and guidance. When a dear brother calls you, respond without question. There is much to be done throughout the world. There must be a harmonious blending of the talents of all those blessed with the Holy Spirit. Each will have a special gift to contribute to this great undertaking in God's work in these latter days.

"The time is short I say again and again and again. These are not idle words. People must be made to realize this. You are to make this urgency known through those with the Holy Spirit. Then the message will fan out and reach all peoples everywhere. All must be given their chance to accept Jesus and the Cross before it is too late. *Stress the lateness of the hour in everything you do for the Lord and in all your testimony, preaching, and witnessing.* Those not saved must be reached by every method and means and channel available to man. They must be told of the shortness of time in which to make their decision for Jesus Christ, Savior and Redeemer. Talk of this message whenever you are able.

"Our Heavenly Father is grieved because many alive today will not be saved because they foolishly think there is ample time remaining for salvation. In this, I repeat, they are wrong. Time is very short. The day of reckoning is near. The fulfillment of the Divine Plan is nigh at hand. Let all heed and turn toward the Cross. Man's blindness to this message will be his undoing. His eyes must be opened, and the light of our dear Lord Jesus must shine through to his soul and consciousness. The Holy Spirit will lead and guide in this movement of the Lord. Give Him free reign and surrender and be obedient to His instructions. This is a clear call for action by all Spirit-filled people everywhere to move in God's work."

Since this prophetic word was given, the Lord has twice impressed me in rather special ways concerning the urgency of our day and hour and our responsibility to redeem the time.

One night I dreamed I was seated in the biology laboratory where I was teaching. I was located about three rows from the front and was in the role of a student rather than that of an instructor. The teacher in my dream was not at the instructor's desk in a place of leadership as he should have been, but was seated back with the students to my left.

I remember I was speaking to the class, but it wasn't about biology; it was about Jesus! I was trying to convey how much the Father loves His Son and how He wants us to love Him, too. Furthermore, He desires that we express that love to each other and to the whole world and thereby prepare the way for His second coming.

It was with great feeling and conviction that these thoughts were being shared. As I was speaking, I felt as if there was very little response within the class. I looked around and everybody, including the instructor, was sound asleep with their heads resting upon their arms which were folded flat upon the tables. I wanted to cry out, "Wake up! Oh, wake up! How can you sleep at a time like this?"

In the morning I remembered the dream most vividly and the Lord brought to my attention a related passage from Scripture. This same portion from God's Word was independently confirmed four times over by different individuals throughout the following week. It is found in Ephesians 5:14-18:

"Therefore, He says, Awake, O sleeper, and arise from the dead, and Christ shall shine [make day dawn] upon you and give you light. Look carefully then how you walk! Live purposefully and worthily and accurately, not as the unwise and witless, but as wise—sensible, intelligent people; Making the very most of the time—buying up each opportunity—because the days are evil.

"Therefore, do not be vague and thoughtless and foolish, but understanding, and firmly grasping what the will of the Lord is. And do not get drunk with wine, for that is debauchery; but ever be filled and stimulated with the (Holy) Spirit" (*Amplified Bible*).

The second time the Lord dealt with me in a rather special way was also in the night. I was clearly awake, and most sensitive to His still, small voice. I recall I was deeply impressed with the urgency of our times. The Lord indicated to me that He was going to be working more swiftly and extensively through His people than ever before.

Furthermore, I was impressed that God was going to be doing surprising things, in surprising ways, in surprising places, through surprising people. In fact, everyone would be surprised in one way or another! No one has the entire view concerning the magnitude of God's end-time ministry through His people. I was cautioned within not to imply to others that the part that I had perceived was the whole, nor was I ever to conclude that the vision anyone else might have would embrace the entirety of God's plan. In this way we remain humbly dependent upon the Lord and His ministry through each other.

As we continue to walk with Him in faith and obedience, He promises to reveal to us what we need to know concerning our role in

His plan—as we need to know it. If we try to force our way into the future, apart from God's Spirit and His Word, we will only be giving place to a spirit of mystical speculation which inevitably leads into error.

In view of such exhortation from the Lord, may we daily consecrate and dedicate our lives to God's holy will without reservation. May we expectantly listen to His voice of instruction and then obediently follow our Heavenly and Holy Shepherd in the path of purity and power. "Even so, come Lord Jesus!

To be filled with the Holy Spirit is to be filled with purifying hope.

9

The Spirit of Joy and Peace

THE JOY OF THE LORD IS YOUR STRENGTH

One of the streams of the Spirit which God is restoring to His Church is the river of joy. Indeed, the Holy Spirit Himself is a very joyful person! There are literally hundreds of references to joy in the Scriptures to confirm this observation. One of the strangest passages is found in Acts 13:52, where we are informed the disciples were full of joy and the Holy Ghost. What is odd about this reference is the context in which this joy was expressed. Paul and Barnabas had just experienced persecution at the hands of the "devout and honorable women and chief men of the city" and had been expelled from the area. Hardly an occasion for joy! Obviously it was not the setting that was the source of their joy, but an overflowing relationship in the joy of the Holy Spirit.

There is a principle here which applies to all of the fruit and graces of the Spirit: that is, they grow best from the ground of adversity. For instance, when the Apostle Paul requested that his "thorn in the flesh" be removed, the Lord informed him that true spiritual *strength* is made perfect in the midst of human *weakness* (II Cor. 12:9). There appears to be a spiritual law of opposites defined here which indicates that *the heavenly streams of the Spirit spring forth most vigorously from the earthly ground of contrasting circumstances.* It is in restless times that we discover His rest; in turmoil, that we find peace; in irritation, that we know patience; in resentment, that we perfect forgiveness; and in distress, that we experience joy.

Jesus said we could be ever- and over-flowing Christians if we would continually trust and obey Him! (John 7:37-39; Acts 5:32). Once when my wife and I were undergoing a rather distressing time the Lord used the occasion to further our understanding of this promise. We had just moved and had become involved in just about everything with which I vowed we would never again become entangled. It was necessary for my wife, who is a nurse, to work the three-to-eleven shift full time. I was endeavoring to establish a new science department with many unforeseen disappointments. The evenings were hectic with the four children when their mother was away. Furthermore, we had just put in a new lawn on sloping banks which kept washing out with each thunderstorm! (I can still remember lying in bed and "rebuking the elements" as the first big drops of an impending storm began to fall. Somehow my frustrated faith never quite held the heavens back.)

One night the Lord gave me a dream in which I was among a group of people all of whom had just made a change in location. Someone suggested we all share what we felt the spiritual purpose was for our respective moves. My heart sank, for it was one of those times when you hope no one will call on you to pray. When my turn came, my mind was distressingly blank until I opened my mouth in faith and in essence these prophetic words tumbled out: "This is a time of preparation in which each of us is enrolled in the school of the Spirit. We are not to face our daily afflictions with resentment, for this is the basic material God is using in shaping our lives into His image. Each day holds a heavenly lesson and an earthly exam. As we cooperate with the Master, it is our privilege to 'rejoice evermore, in all things.' "

Our joy and every other fruit of the Spirit does not have its source in our circumstances or from our feelings, but in Jesus. As we make this our confession, the Holy Spirit can bring a confirming witness to our hearts. There is something strong and steady in this kind of joy because it is based on the faithfulness of the Lord rather than the fluctuation of our feelings or the uncertainty of our surroundings. As one man expressed it, *"It is a kind of solid joy, and it brings a staying power to our lives!"*

PEACE BE UNTO YOU

The fast, feverish, high-pressured pace of our modern world has produced an atmosphere which is not conducive to inner peace of heart. Far too often our lives are characterized by an inner agitation or restlessness of soul. Stress, strain, fear, and worry make their marks, and man's soul cries out for relief. It is even possible for the spiri of this age to spill over into our Christian life, and we can become so frantic in our service for the Lord that we succeed more in wearing ourselves out than in gaining solid ground for God in our lives or in the lives of others.

For the Spirit-filled Christian, however, there is the promise of inner peace and rest. There is a serenity of mind and repose for the soul which enables us to maintain a spiritual poise regardless of circumstances. Real life demands more than pretty promises and sweet sentiment. There must be a solid center to our lives which remains unmoved and untouched by the storms of life and the turmoil of our times. *That center is Christ!*

Let us explore this in a more specific way. Peace and rest are far more than just abstract characteristics of the Christian life. These words are more than just wishful thoughts or expressions of soft sentiment. Each one is a reference to something which is as solid as concrete and as strong as tempered steel. That something is really Someone. *That Someone is Jesus Christ!* Jesus Christ is what makes our Christianity concrete. When the Holy Spirit fills us with the Life of our Lord, He is putting steel into our soul. Peace is a Person; rest is a Person. *That Person is Jesus Christ.* He is the solid center of our lives!

Now we can only stay "on center" when we by faith allow the Holy Spirit to have full and complete control of our lives. If we are restless or lose our inner harmony of heart, we have moved "off center" in some area of our experience. All we have to do is ask the Holy Spirit to *recentralize* our lives. This He will do by many ways and means. Usually, He will simply begin with us, and suggest that we acquaint now ourselves with Him and be at peace (Job 22:21). It is impossible to get better acquainted with Jesus and not be at peace because *He is peace!* It is the desire of the blessed Comforter to help us get better acquainted with Jesus just at such times as we need Him most.

The pathway of God's will is the pathway of peace! Here is a very positive principle that should give direction to every Spirit-filled believer. If any situation destroys your inner harmony of heart, quiet yourself before Him. Ask the Holy Spirit of truth to reveal to you if something is off-center. It may be your doubts (misplaced faith). Ask God to square your faith with Scripture. Center your trust in His Word. To trust His Word when feelings and even reason may indicate otherwise will bring His peace.

On the other hand, your uneasiness may be a sense of discernment that Jesus is not finding the place He desires to have. Any situation which does not direct our full attention to the Lord is partially off-center. A truly Christ-centered life will quickly detect this. It may begin merely as a feeling of uneasiness, but as we seek God's Spirit to relate things to Jesus, He will bring discernment of a more specific nature!

The principle of peace finds very practical application when we face the many decisions which confront us in everyday life. *Every day is a day of decision!* Sometimes they are little decisions and sometimes big decisions that can change our entire lives. If we learn how to make the little decisions, we will know how to face the big ones. The way in which we face the decisions of today may well determine those of tomorrow.

For the Spirit-filled Christian, this way is the way of peace. Without inner peace of heart it is impossible to sense God's will or hear His voice. Sometimes His voice is very still and very small—purposefully so! The inner noise of confusion and unrest will completely drown it out. The remedy for such inner distress is simply the presence of Christ. One touch of His hand can calm the troubled waters of our soul.

How easy it is for us to stray from the way of peace. But when we do, we hear a word behind us saying, "This is the way, walk ye in it" (Isa. 30:21). Jesus tenderly reminds us that *He is that way* (John 14:6). Upon returning to Him we find inner rest, and in such quietness and confidence we find inner strength (Isa. 30:15). *It is as we rest in Him that we can go forth in His name!* (II Chron. 14:11). Let us therefore acquaint ourselves with Him and be at peace (Job 22:21). And, "Let the peace (soul harmony which comes) from the Christ rule . . . in your hearts—deciding and settling with finality all questions that arise in your minds—[in that peaceful state] . . . be thankful—appreciative, giving praise to God always" (Col. 3:15 *Amplified Bible*).

To be filled with the Spirit is to be filled with joy and peace!

10

The Spirit of Love

What better topic could we choose with which to conclude our time in sharing together than that of love. God is love! We see His love expressed for us in Jesus. Calvary love is much more than sweet sentiment. It is the very heartbeat of God. *Love not only is; it gives!* The Father gave us His heart when He gave us His Son. He exhausted the very treasury of heaven that we might have fellowship with Him. In ourselves we are not worthy of His love, but He loves us anyway!

The love of John 3:16 is expressed by the Greek word "agape." It is the highest and noblest word for love. In the New Testament it takes on a divine dimension that gives it an infinite value. It is the kind of love that is characterized by the subject loving—God. It is further characterized by the value and preciousness of the object loved—you and me. God considers us to be of infinite value because of the divine purpose for which we were created—that we might be conformed into the image of His Son. *Agape love is calvary love!*

The Holy Spirit is the Spirit of love. His overwhelming desire is to fill us with the love that God is. "For God's love has been poured out in our hearts through the Holy Spirit Who has been given to us" (Rom. 5:5 *Amplified Bible*).

THE LOVELY GIFTS OF GOD

The fruit and the gifts of the Spirit are expressions of God's love. The fruit of the Spirit (Gal. 5:22-23) is but a variation of love in its *being* or *character.* Love, joy, gladness, peace, are what love is *within;* longsuffering, patience, gentleness, goodness are what love is *toward man;* faithfulness, meekness (humility), temperance (self-control) are what love is *toward God.*

The gifts of the Spirit as found in I Corinthians 12:8-10 are expressions of God's love in *thought, word* and *deed.* Wisdom, knowledge, discernment are love in *thought;* prophecy, tongues, interpretations are love in *word;* faith, healings, miracles are love in *deed.*

To consider the gifts as expressions of God's life and love assists us in responding to the Spirit in faith when it comes to their manifestation. If we deliberately place ourselves before the Lord in expectation (choosing to be chosen), He has an available and cooperative vessel through which He can carry His love to another. *Our desire will be to share God's life and love, and actively allow the Spirit to minister through us in some specific way.* As we submit our spirit to His in faith, we will expectantly endeavor to think and feel as He would in our situation. As we become aware of His mind and affection, then it is our responsibility to express His will and feeling to God's people. This may also involve doing in faith what He would do if He were in our shoes—and He is! "As thou hast sent me into the world, even so have I also sent them into the world" (John 17:18).

Even those who through experience have learned "to excel" in the lovely expression of the spiritual gifts had to begin at the bottom. *There is a "first time" for everybody to try his spiritual wings.* The endeavor to put into words what we sense in the Spirit that God would say in a given situation can become sweetly inspired prophecy, a word of wisdom, or interpretation. Prayer in faith and in spiritual compassion (which is more than sympathy) can produce the climate for the demonstration of: healings, miracles, and faith—all powerful expressions of God's love!

Some manifestations of the gifts seem to have a high order of inspiration and to be very sovereignly expressed. Other manifestations of the Spirit may occur or begin in what seems such a natural way we don't realize the inspiration involved until we see the obvious conclusion. Let us so live in the Spirit that God can move through us in the gifts whether we are aware of it or not. "A word fitly spoken is like apples of gold in pictures of silver" (Prov. 25:11). Here is a beautiful picture of a divine word of wisdom set in God's redeeming love. *May we be trees of life daily producing apples of gold for those who seek God's truth in love.*

Without the full complement of the fruit and gifts of the Spirit, God's love is incomplete to and through His Church. With the present outpouring of the Holy Spirit, we are seeing the Spirit of love completing His ministry in the Church. This is how the Church is to become as fresh and full of promise as the morning; as fair as the still, cool beauty of the moon; as bright as the warm revealing sun; and as terrible as an aggressive victorious army with banners (Song of Sol. 6:10). *Love is fresh, fair, bright, and powerful!* Does not Calvary speak of promise, rest, light, and victory? This is the gospel of the Cross. This is our message to a hopeless, restless, darkened, sin-shackled world. Through His love God has provided deliverance for body, soul, and spirit. Can we do any less than shout to a dying world, "Look to His love and live!"

LONELY AND UNLOVED

Everywhere there are hearts literally longing for God's love! I remember two very vivid experiences related to this. One concerned a young seminary student who was interested in the baptism with the Holy Spirit for his life. We had talked with him for a while and were about to pray together when he broke down and pleaded with me to pray that God would somehow reveal to him His love. I can still feel and hear the desperate cry of his heart as he longed to know that God loved him *personally.* The Holy Spirit prompted me with a word of wisdom which I immediately shared with him. "How could God any more clearly and forcefully show His great love for you, personally, than He did when He gave His own Son?"

Calvary love is terribly real, and he responded immediately to this real assurance that God graciously provided. How long he had carried this burden I do not know, but I somehow feel that there are many lonely lives, some whom we may least suspect, that are likewise longing for an assurance that God loves them.

On another occasion we were counseling with the wife of a pastor who was interested in the fullness of God's Spirit for her life. In the course of our prayer together the Lord brought a brief prophecy concerning His interest, concern, and love for her. "Oh," she cried, "does God *really* love me? For a whole year I have been going through a valley of darkness and have wondered many times if God still loved me." This assurance of God's love to which the Holy Spirit witnessed brought peace and joy to her heart.

There is no greater privilege than to share the love of Jesus with others! May His Spirit so fill our lives with the love of God that anytime, anyplace, anywhere, others may be able to look to us and know that God loves them. May we join with Rufus Moseley at this point and again repeat his rather charming comment, "Jesus really loves you, and He told me to tell you so!"

We now share with you this last thought, and really it is the most important of all for everything else rests upon it:

To be filled with the Holy Spirit is to be filled with Calvary Love!

Appendix

Appendix

A CORRELATION OF SCRIPTURE RELATING

THE PERSON OF THE HOLY SPIRIT TO THE

LIFE OF THE BELIEVER

"And ye shall seek me, and find me, when ye shall search for me with all your heart." (Jer. 29:13)

"They received the word with all readiness of mind, and searched the scriptures daily, whether those things were so." (Acts 17:11)

I. PERSONAL PROMISES FOR HOLY SPIRIT BAPTISM

1. And it shall come to pass afterward, that I will pour out my spirit upon all flesh; and your sons and your daughters shall prophesy, your old men shall dream dreams, your young men shall see visions: And also upon the servants and upon the handmaids in those days will I pour out my spirit. (Joel 2:28-29)

2.   In those days came John the Baptist, preaching in the wilderness of Judaea, And saying, Repent ye: for the kingdom of heaven is at hand. . . . I indeed baptize you with water unto repentance: but he [Jesus] that cometh after me is mightier than I, whose shoes I am not worthy to bear: he shall baptize you with the Holy Ghost, and with fire: (Matt. 3:1-2, 11)

3.   He that believeth on me [Jesus], as the scripture hath said, out of his belly shall flow rivers of living water.(But this spake he of the Spirit, which they that believe on him should receive: for the Holy Ghost was not yet given; because that Jesus was not yet glorified.) (John 7:38-39)

4.   And I [Jesus] will pray the Father, and he shall give you another Comforter, that he may abide with you for ever; Even the Spirit of truth; whom the world cannot receive, because it seeth him not, neither knoweth him: but ye know him; for he dwelleth with you, and shall be in you.
        The Comforter, which is the Holy Ghost, whom the Father will send in my name, he shall teach you all things, and bring all things to your remembrance, whatsoever I have said unto you. (John 14:16-17, 26)

5.   But when the Comforter is come, whom I [Jesus] will send unto you from the Father, even the Spirit of truth, which proceedeth from the Father, he shall testify of me: (John 15:26)

6.   Nevertheless I [Jesus] tell you the truth; It is expedient for you that I go away: for if I go not away, the Comforter will not come unto you; but if I depart, I will send him unto you.
        I have yet many things to say unto you, but ye cannot bear them now. Howbeit when he, the Spirit of truth, is come, he will guide you into all truth: for he shall not speak of himself; but whatsoever he shall hear, that shall he speak: and he will shew you things to come. He shall glorify me: for he shall receive of mine, and shall shew it unto you. (John 16:7, 12-14)

7.   And, being assembled together with them, [Jesus] commanded them [the disciples] that they should not depart from Jerusalem, but wait for the promise of the Father, which, saith he, ye have heard of me. For John truly baptized with water; but ye shall be baptized with the Holy Ghost not many days hence.

Ye shall receive power, after that the Holy Ghost is come upon you: and ye shall be witnesses unto me, both in Jerusalem, and in all Judaea, and in Samaria, and unto the uttermost part of the earth. (Acts 1:4-5, 8)

II. THE PROMISES PERSONALLY FULFILLED

1.   And when the day of Pentecost was fully come, they [the disciples] were all with one accord in one place. And suddenly there came a sound from heaven as of a rushing mighty wind, and it filled all the house where they were sitting. And there appeared unto them cloven tongues like as of fire, and it sat upon each of them. And they were all filled with the Holy Ghost, and began to speak with other tongues, as the Spirit gave them utterance.

Now when this was noised abroad, the multitude came together, and were confounded, because that every man heard them speak in his own language. And they were all amazed and marvelled, saying one to another, Behold, are not all these which speak Galilaeans? . . . We do hear them speak in our tongues the wonderful works of God. And they were all amazed, and were in doubt, saying one to another, What meaneth this? Others mocking said, These men are full of new wine. (Acts 2:1-4, 6-7, 11-13)

2.   But Peter, standing up with the eleven, lifted up his voice, and said unto them, Ye men of Judaea, and all ye that dwell at Jerusalem, be this known unto you, and hearken to my words: For these are not drunken, as ye suppose, seeing it is but the third hour of the day.

But this is that which was spoken by the prophet Joel; And it shall come to pass in the last days saith God, I will pour out of my Spirit upon all flesh: and your sons and your daughters shall prophesy, and your young men shall see visions, and your old men shall dream dreams: And on my servants and on my handmaidens I will pour out in those days of my Spirit; and they shall prophesy: (Acts 2:14-18)

3.   Ye men of Israel, hear these words; Jesus of Nazareth, a man approved of God among you by miracles and wonders and signs, which God did by him in the midst of you, as ye yourselves

also know: Him, being delivered by the determinate counsel and foreknowledge of God, ye have taken, and by wicked hands have crucified and slain: . . . This Jesus hath God raised up, whereof we all are witnesses. Therefore, being by the right hand of God exalted, and having received of the Father the promise of the Holy Ghost, he hath shed forth this, which ye now see and hear. (Acts 2:22-23, 32-33)

III.   THE PATTERN FOR PERSONAL FULFILLMENT

1.   Now when they heard this, they were pricked in their heart, and said unto Peter and to the rest of the apostles, Men and brethren, what shall we do? Then Peter said unto them, Repent, and be baptized every one of you in the name of Jesus Christ for the remission of sins, and ye shall receive the gift of the Holy Ghost. For the promise is unto you, and to your children, and to all that are afar off, even as many as the Lord our God shall call. . . . Then they that gladly received his word were baptized: and the same day there were added unto them about three thousand souls. (Acts 2:37-39, 41)

2.   Then Philip went down to the city of Samaria, and preached Christ unto them. . . . But when they believed Philip preaching of the things concerning the kingdom of God, and the name of Jesus Christ, they were baptized, both men and women.

Now when the apostles which were at Jerusalem heard that Samaria had received the word of God, they sent unto them Peter and John: Who, when they were come down, prayed for them, that they might receive the Holy Ghost: (For as yet he was fallen upon none of them: only they were baptized in the name of the Lord Jesus.) Then laid they their hands on them, and they received the Holy Ghost. (Acts 8:5, 12, 14-17)

3.   And Ananias went his way, and entered into the house; and putting his hands on him said, Brother Saul, the Lord, even Jesus, that appeared unto thee in the way as thou camest, hath sent me, that thou mightest receive thy sight, and be filled with the Holy Ghost. And immediately there fell from his eyes as it had been scales: and he received sight forthwith, and arose, and was baptized. (Acts 9:17-18)

4. And as Peter was coming in, Cornelius [a devout gentile centurion] met him, and fell down at his feet, and worshipped him. But Peter took him up, saying, Stand up; I myself also am a man. And as he talked with him, he went in, and found many that were come together. And he said unto them, Ye know how that it is an unlawful thing for a man that is a Jew to keep company, or come unto one of another nation; but God hath showed me that I should not call any man common or unclean.

Then Peter opened his mouth, and said, Of a truth I perceive that God is no respecter of persons: But in every nation he that feareth him, and worketh righteousness, is accepted with him. The word which God sent unto the children of Israel, preaching peace by Jesus Christ: (he is Lord of all:) That word, I say, ye know, which was published throughout all Judaea, and began from Galilee, after the baptism which John preached; How God anointed Jesus of Nazareth with the Holy Ghost and with power: who went about doing good, and healing all that were oppressed of the devil; for God was with him.

And we are witnesses of all things which he did both in the land of the Jews, and in Jerusalem; whom they slew and hanged on a tree: Him God raised up the third day, and shewed him openly; Not to all the people, but unto witnesses chosen before of God, even to us, who did eat and drink with him after he rose from the dead. And he commanded us to preach unto the people, and to testify that it is he which was ordained of God to be the Judge of the quick and the dead. To him give all the prophets witness, that through his name whosoever believeth in him shall receive remission of sins.

While Peter yet spake these words, the Holy Ghost fell on all them which heard the word. And they of the circumcision [Jews] which believed were astonished, as many as came with Peter, because that on the Gentiles also was poured out the gift of the Holy Ghost. For they heard them speak with tongues, and magnify God. Then answered Peter, Can any man forbid water, that these should not be baptized, which have received the Holy Ghost as well as we? And he commanded them to be baptized in the name of the Lord. Then prayed they him to tarry certain days. (Acts 10:25-28, 34-48)

5. And the apostles and [Jewish] brethren that were in Judaea heard that the Gentiles had also received the word of God. And

when Peter was come up to Jerusalem, they that were of the circumcision contended with him, Saying Thou wentest in to men uncircumcised, and didst eat with them.

But Peter rehearsed the matter from the beginning, and expounded it by order unto them, saying ... And as I began to speak [to the Gentiles], the Holy Ghost fell on them, as on us at the beginning. Then remembered I the word of the Lord, how that he said, John indeed baptized with water; but ye shall be baptized with the Holy Ghost. Forasmuch then as God gave them the like gift as he did unto us, who believed on the Lord Jesus Christ; what was I, that I could withstand God? When they heard these things, they held their peace, and glorified God ... (Acts 11:1-4, 15-18)

6.   And it came to pass, that, while Apollos was at Corinth, Paul having passed through the upper coasts came to Ephesus: and finding certain disciples, He said unto them, Have ye received the Holy Ghost since ye believed? And they said unto him, We have not so much as heard whether there be any Holy Ghost. And he said unto them, Unto what then were ye baptized? And they said, Unto John's baptism. Then said Paul, John verily baptized with the baptism of repentance, saying unto the people, that they should believe on him which should come after him, that is, on Christ Jesus.

When they heard this, they were baptized in the name of the Lord Jesus. And when Paul had laid his hands upon them, the Holy Ghost came on them; and they spake with tongues and prophesied. And all the men were about twelve. (Acts 19:1-7)

IV.   PERSONALLY APPROPRIATED BY FAITH

1.   This only would I [Paul] learn of you, Received ye the Spirit by the works of the law, or by the hearing of faith?

That the blessing of Abraham might come on the Gentiles through Jesus Christ; that we might receive the promise of the Spirit through faith. (Gal. 3:2, 14)

2.   He that believeth on me [Jesus], as the scripture hath said, out of his belly shall flow rivers of living water. (But this spake he of the Spirit, which they that believe on him should receive; for

the Holy Ghost was not yet given; because that Jesus was not yet glorified.) (John 7:38-39)

3.   And I [Jesus] say unto you, Ask, and it shall be given you; seek, and ye shall find; knock, and it shall be opened unto you. For everyone that asketh receiveth; and he that seeketh findeth; and to him that knocketh, it shall be opened.

If a son shall ask bread of any of you that is a father, will he give him a stone? or if he ask a fish, will he for a fish give him a serpent? Or if he shall ask an egg, will he offer him a scorpion? If ye then, being evil, know how to give good gifts unto your children: how much more shall your heavenly Father give the Holy Spirit to them that ask him? (Luke 11:9-13)

V.   THE PRIVILEGE OF INSPIRED PRAYER AND PRAISE FOR PERSONAL DEVOTIONS

1.   After my words they spake not again; and my speech dropped upon them. And they waited for me as for the rain; and they opened their mouths wide as for the latter rain. (Job 29:22-23)

2.   Open thy mouth wide, and I will fill it. (Psa. 81:10)

3.   For with stammering lips and another tongue will he speak to this people. To whom he said, This is the rest wherewith ye may cause the weary to rest; and this is the refreshing: yet they would not hear. (Isa. 28:11-12)

4.   And they were all filled with the Holy Ghost, and began to speak with other tongues, as the Spirit gave them utterance. (Acts 2:4)

5.   While Peter yet spake these words, the Holy Ghost fell on all them which heard the word. For they heard them speak with tongues, and magnify God. (Acts 10:44, 46)

6.   And when Paul had laid his hands upon them, the Holy Ghost came on them; and they spake with tongues. (Acts 19:6)

7.   And these signs shall follow them that believe; In my name shall they cast out devils; they shall speak with new tongues. (Mark 16:17)

8.   I [Paul] thank my God, I speak with tongues more than ye all [in private devotions] ... [For] He that speaketh in an unknown tongue edifieth himself ... [and] verily givest thanks well ... he that speaketh in an unknown tongue, speaketh not unto men, but unto God: for no man understandeth him; howbeit in the spirit he speaketh mysteries.... For if I pray in an unknown tongue, my spirit prayeth, but my understanding is unfruitful. (I Cor. 14:18, 4, 17, 2, 14)

9.   The Spirit also helpeth our infirmities: for we know not what we should pray for as we ought: but the Spirit itself maketh intercession for us with groanings which cannot be uttered. And he that searcheth the hearts knoweth what is the mind of the Spirit, because he maketh intercession for the saints according to the will of God. (Rom. 8:26-27)

10.   But ye, beloved, building up yourselves on your most holy faith, praying in the Holy Ghost. (Jude 20)

11.   Praying always with all prayer and supplication in the Spirit, and watching thereunto with all perseverance and supplication for all saints. (Ephesians 6:18)

12.   By him therefore let us offer the sacrifice of praise to God continually, that is, the fruit of our lips giving thanks to his name. (Heb. 13:15)

13.   Let my prayer be set forth before thee as incense: and the lifting up of my hands as the evening sacrifice. (Psa. 141:2)

14.   For they heard them speak with tongues, and magnify God. (Acts 10:46)

15.   O magnify the Lord with me, and let us exalt his name together. (Psa. 34:3)

16.   I will bless the Lord at all times: his praise shall continually be in my mouth. (Psa. 34:1)

VI. MARKS OF THE SPIRIT-FILLED CHRISTIAN

1. And they were all *filled* with the Holy Ghost, and began to speak with other tongues, as the Spirit gave them utterance. (Acts 2:4)

2. And now, Lord, behold their threatenings: and grant unto thy servants, that with all boldness they may speak thy word, By stretching forth thine hand to heal; and that signs and wonders may be done by the name of thy holy child Jesus.
   And when they had prayed, the place was shaken where they were assembled together; and they were *filled* with the Holy Ghost, and they spake the word of God with boldness. (Acts 4:29-31)

3. Wherefore, brethren, look ye out among you seven men of honest report, *full* of the Holy Ghost and wisdom, whom we may appoint over this business. (Acts 6:3)

4. And the saying pleased the whole multitude: and they chose Stephen, a man *full* of faith and of the Holy Ghost . . . And Stephen full of faith and power, did great wonders and miracles among the people. (Acts 6:5, 8)

5. And the disciples were *filled* with joy, and with the Holy Ghost. (Acts 13:52)

6. Now the God of hope *fill* you with all joy and peace in believing, that ye may abound in hope, through the power of the Holy Ghost. (Rom. 15:13)

7. And be not drunk with wine, wherein is excess; but be *filled* with the Spirit; Speaking to yourselves in psalms and hymns and spiritual songs, singing and making melody in your heart to the Lord: Giving thanks always for all things unto God and the Father in the name of our Lord Jesus Christ. (Eph. 5:18-20)

Robert C. Frost is author of *Aglow with the Spirit* published by Logos International. A step-by-step account both from scriptural and personal testimony of the author's discovery of Jesus Christ as the Baptizer in the Holy Spirit.

Available in bookstores or from Logos Publishers, Plainfield, New Jersey 07060.

SUGGESTED INEXPENSIVE PAPERBACK BOOKS
WHEREVER PAPERBACKS ARE SOLD
OR USE ORDER FORM.

THE ARMSTRONG ERROR by Charles DeLoach L317/95¢
A reporter investigates Herbert W. Armstrong and The World Tomorrow broadcast and the Plain Truth movement.

LOST SHEPHERD by Agnes Sandford L328/95¢
First time in paperback after 7 printings in hard cover. The accounts of a minister's search for a dynamic ministry and a woman with an unconventional healing ministry.

AGLOW WITH THE SPIRIT
by Dr. Robert Frost L326/95¢
A scientist shows his spiritual discovery of the baptism in the Holy Spirit.

WALK IN THE SPIRIT by Michael Harper L319/95¢
There is a place where there is a life to live through the Holy Spirit.

COMING ALIVE by Jamie Buckingham L305/1.75
YOUR NEW LOOK by Jamie Buckingham L306/1.75
COMING ALIVE is a book written for parents and children with pre-Junior High level, presenting a Christian view of sex information. YOUR NEW LOOK is for the Junior High age-level.

15 STEPS OUT by Bob Mumford L106/1.50
Vital questions of practical living and choosing and knowing what is the correct way to select the spiritual ways offered.

OVERFLOWING LIFE by Robert Frost L327/1.75
The exciting fulfillment of a spirit-filled life. The experiences expected after the baptism in the Holy Spirit.

THE SOUL PATROL by Bob Bartlett L308/1.95
A gripping account of teen challenge in Philadelphia, its birth and outreach to addicts, dropouts and problem youth.

FOR INSPIRATIONAL READING

POWER IN PRAISE L-342/1.95
Merlin Corothers

RUN BABY RUN by Nicky Cruz L-101/75¢
The true story of a gang leader turned crusader.

THE CHALLENGING COUNTERFEIT
by Raphael Gasson L-102/75¢
Hidden secrets of spiritualism disclosed by a former medium who tells
how to know the real.

ANGELS OF LIGHT? by Dr. Hobart Freeman L-103/1.50
Dr. Freeman reveals the source of power in the popular occult practices
and the deliverence from them.

EMOTIONAL ILLS AND THE CHRISTIAN
by G. J. Guldseth, M. D. L-116/1.50
A high percentage of illness is attributed to the psychosomatic.
Dr. Guldseth discusses ways of healing through the Bible.

PRISON TO PRAISE
by Chaplain (LTC) M. Carothers L-302/1.50
Revolutionary concepts in achieving remarkable answers to
problems through praise.

THE SPIRIT BADE ME GO
by David duPlessis L-325/95¢
A charismatic journey of one man bringing him before thousands in a
worldwide ecumenical mission for the Holy Spirit.

WISE UP! HOW? by Clinton White L-318/95¢
"I was an alcoholic fourteen years and addicted to drugs. I was set
free. I call it a miracle."

- - - - - WHEREVER PAPERBACKS ARE SOLD OR USE THIS COUPON - - - - -

LOGOS BOOKS
Dept. LP, 185 North Avenue, Plainfield, NJ 07060

Please send me the INSPIRATIONAL books circled below.
I enclose $_____ ▫ sample copy LOGOS JOURNAL

L101   L102   L103   L116   L302   L325   L-342

L318   L317   L328   L326   L319   L305

L306   L106   L327   ▫ Cassette #_____
▫ Book catalog L308

Name _____
Street _____
City_____ **State**_____ **Zip**_____
▫ Sample copy of LOGOS JOURNAL